The Courts of Law
A guide to their history and working

Peter N. Walker

The Courts of Law

A guide to their history and working

DAVID AND CHARLES : NEWTON ABBOT

ISBN 0 7153 4977 5

COPYRIGHT NOTICE

Set in 11/12 Pilgrim
and printed in Great Britain
by Bristol Typesetting Company Limited
for David & Charles (Publishers) Limited
South Devon House Newton Abbot Devon

Contents

	AUTHOR'S NOTE	7
ONE	INTRODUCTION	9
	Origins of the law . the oath . classification of offences	
TWO	THE HIGH COURTS	17
	The House of Lords . Queen's Bench Division of the High Court . the Central Criminal Court . the Crown Courts of Liverpool and Manchester . the assizes . procedure at a criminal assize court (including crown courts, Central Criminal Court and quarter sessions) . the jury	
THREE	MAGISTRATES AND THEIR COURTS	46
	Magistrates . quarter sessions . magistrates' courts . examining magistrates . domestic courts . juvenile courts	
FOUR	CIVIL COURTS	75
	The county courts . bankruptcy courts . Chancery Division of the High Court . Probate, Divorce and Admiralty Division of the High Court . civil court procedure	
FIVE	CORONERS	102
	History . informing the coroner . before the inquest . at the inquest . treasure trove	
SIX	APPEALS, LEGAL AID AND BAIL	125

SEVEN MISCELLANEOUS COURTS   149
       The Court of Chivalry . courts leet . uni-
       versity courts . the Palatine Courts of Lan-
       caster and Durham . Court of Record for the
       Hundred of Salford . the Liverpool Court of
       Passage . Court of Protection . Restrictive
       Practices Court . Tolzey Court of Bristol
       and Court of Pie Powder . the forest courts .
       ecclesiastical courts . the Trial of the Pyx

EIGHT OBSOLETE COURTS   174
       Curia Regis . General Eyre . Court of Com-
       mon Pleas . the Royal Courts of Justice . the
       Court of Requests . Court of Star Chamber .
       Exchequer Court

       SHORT GLOSSARY OF LEGAL TERMS   183

       BIBLIOGRAPHY   197

       INDEX   199

Author's Note

The average person, whose work and life seldom involves him with a court of law, is often puzzled by the English courts. There are so many of them and each performs a different function, with its own rules and procedure. The distinction between civil and criminal law is not easily understood and another puzzling feature is that some crimes can be dealt with at a magistrates' court while others must be tried at the assizes or quarter sessions.

This book has been written in an attempt to assist the layman with this sort of problem, and to help him understand some of the functions of the English legal system. It is not intended for the practitioner for whom most of the contents will be common knowledge.

The history of the various courts is briefly included in the hope that this will help the reader to appreciate their development and jurisdiction, but lack of space has demanded brevity.

ONE

Introduction

ORIGINS OF THE LAW

To understand the functions of the legal system, it is necessary to know something of the origins of the law. Law can be defined as a body of rules of conduct which are recognised and enforced in courts of law and by which the conduct of the community is ordered and controlled.

So far as legal systems are concerned, England is perhaps unique because of its adherence to common law; certain other nations, like Australia, enjoy a similar system introduced by English settlers and which is based upon the English common law system. Common law is unique because it is not in statute form. It consists of an unwritten code of conduct which has evolved over the centuries and which has been accepted as standard practice by successive generations. As society became more sophisticated, however, efforts were made to introduce written laws. Edward the Confessor (1042-66) tried, and William I tried again in 1070. This seems to be the start of statute law, which is made by direct order of the State, set down in writing in Acts of Parliament and given royal assent before coming into force.

Today, common law persists alongside statute law; as early as 1236 a statute declared that the nobles should not change the laws which had so long been used and this principle has survived to this day. A good example is the crime of conspiracy which is still a common law offence. This was the charge levelled against the Great Train Robbers of 1963: they were not charged under any specific Act of Parliament, but were charged under common law with conspiring to rob a mail train. Because no punishment is specified by common law, the judge was able to inflict sentences of twenty-five or thirty years' imprisonment. There is no such punishment written into the laws of the nation; had the robbers been dealt with under statute law they might have suffered a lesser penalty. Had they been charged with robbery with violence, they could, however, have received life imprisonment under the now repealed Larceny Act, 1916.

It follows that common law is still a very useful weapon in the enforcement of English law. Very recently, a judge said that common law moves with the times, and therefore it can alter to fit a changing society. It is logical that English courts, which have grown from common law, are many and varied. Their origins lie deep in early English history and many of them have obscure or even unknown sources. Nonetheless, they are widely regarded as the finest in the world. Many scholars attribute this to the common law heritage, and to the resultant flexibility of the legal system.

Early common law was enforced in the shire courts and the hundred courts. England was divided into shires, the majority of which have survived into modern times, and their courts met occasionally each year. But each shire was divided into hundreds; these also had their own courts which sat more frequently and, as a very rough guide, a hundred was equivalent to a modern rural district. This makes the functions of a hundred court very akin to those of a modern magistrates' court.

The idea of having a court as a place to settle disputes is as old as the law itself. The word 'court' strictly means a house, particularly that of the sovereign. It quickly grew to include the king plus his followers or his household and became the King's Court. In fact, the term still means the sovereign's household. The sovereign was the nation's judge. He travelled to all parts to see that justice was done and these gatherings of important people became known as courts. When the king eventually passed the responsibility of law enforcement over to his judges, the places where they conducted their trials also became known as courts.

Even today, the responsibilities of the sovereign are encountered in the courts, particularly in charges involving a breach of the peace. This is really the queen's peace, and is the normal state of society: any interruption of it is a breach of the peace. In Norman times, this state of tranquillity was deemed to embrace the entire nation and the logical outcome was that any crime must be a breach of the peace; it was therefore dealt with at the King's Court. Some indictable offences are today charged as being 'against the peace of our sovereign lady the Queen, her Crown and dignity'.

The shire courts and the hundred courts operated at the same time as the King's Court, but they dealt with minor offences against the law. These courts were soon dominated by the landowners who began to dispute the king's authority. To counteract this there developed the system of sending judges into the country to administer justice, where hitherto the king himself had travelled for this purpose.

The judges represented the king and were given all his powers and this is why they are so powerful today; they can order the death penalty which still exists for some offences, such as high treason, arson of HM ships and docks, and piracy with violence. In early times, though, there was little or no difference between criminal and civil proceedings. This caused problems in the early courts so that many of them dealt with matters not strictly within their jurisdiction, but gradually a line was drawn. Today, criminal offences can be described as those which affect the community at large, eg murder, rape, etc, while a dispute between two individuals affects only themselves. This latter case would be settled in a civil court while criminal matters go to a criminal court.

THE OATH

In every court of law an oath to tell the truth is used in an attempt to produce truthful and exact evidence. The Oaths Act of 1888 said that a person must swear on oath on being called to give evidence in court. He could, however, elect to affirm instead if he:

(i) had no religious belief
(ii) believed the taking of the oath was contrary to his religion
(iii) was, or had been, a Quaker or a Moravian.

Before a witness could affirm in court, it was vital that his objection to the oath was based on one of the above provisions. In 1961 these provisions were relaxed. Today an affirmation in lieu of the oath is permitted if it is not practicable to administer an oath appropriate to the witness's religious belief. An affirmation is little more than a promise. It differs from an oath in that it is not accompanied by an invocation to God to witness what is said. In the early days Christians thought they would be struck dead if they told a lie after swearing on oath, and it was for this reason that the oath was used in court. All orthodox Christians, ie Roman Catholics, members of the Greek and Russian Orthodox churches, Anglicans and most other Protestants, still take the Christian oath, though some individuals may object for personal reasons. For example, some Baptists refuse to be sworn, basing their reasons on the gospel according to St Matthew which says 'But I say unto you, swear not at all; neither by heaven for it is God's throne, nor by the earth for it is his footstool.' When taking the Christian oath, a copy of the New Testament is held high in the right hand and the witness says, 'I swear by Almighty God that the evidence I shall give shall be the truth, the whole truth and nothing but the truth.' In a juvenile court, this varies (see page 72). The addendum 'so help me God' is not included in the British oath, although it does appear in American films.

Other religions cling faithfully to their own particular method. Many Jews take the oath with their heads covered; all hold aloft a copy of the Old Testament. Mohammedans swear on the Koran, which is the bible of their faith, and some insist on using their own language. The Buddhist oath reads 'I declare, as in the presence of Buddha, that I am unprejudiced and if what I speak shall prove false, or if by colouring truth others shall be led astray, then may the Three Holy Existences, Buddha, Dhamma and Pro Sangha, in whose sight I now stand, together with the Devotees of the twenty-two Firmaments, punish me and also my migrating soul'.

One of the most unusual methods is that employed by the Chinese, and which can vary according to the part of China from which the witness comes. Some blow out a lighted candle, some sacrifice a white cockerel, but the most common method is to break a saucer. In 1841 a Chinese was lawfully sworn by taking a china saucer in his hands, then shattering it on the rail of the witness box while an officer administered the following oath: 'You shall tell the truth and the whole truth; the saucer is cracked and if you do not tell the truth, your soul will be cracked like the saucer.' All these oaths are equally binding in court, just as the affirmation is binding on a person who has no religion. Such a person will say 'I . . . do solemnly and sincerely and truly declare and affirm that I will tell the truth, the whole truth and nothing but the truth'. A person is lawfully sworn if the court or commissioner before whom he makes his oath, affirmation, or declaration, has the power to administer it, and if it is in such form and with such ceremonies as he accepts without question or declares to be binding upon him.

The Scottish oath is taken without the Bible, and the Welsh Courts (Oaths and Interpreters) Rules 1943 give translations of over twenty oaths and affirmations. Even so, all records in the Welsh courts must be kept in English. When a non-English-speaking person gives evidence in an English court, an interpreter must be present and this person swears or affirms that he will truly interpret and explain to the court all matters or things required of him.

There are many types of oath; the ones given above are used by witnesses who give evidence before the court. There are others used by jurors, coroners and on other occasions.

CLASSIFICATION OF OFFENCES

One puzzling aspect of court procedure is the classification of offences. This classification is important because it determines the place of trial, and there is a clear distinction between civil and criminal offences. In criminal offences it also determines the power to arrest an offender. Whereas the amount of a civil action will determine its venue of trial, there is a more complicated procedure for criminal offenders.

From the earliest days of common law there was a difference between felonies and misdemeanours. The word 'felon' was used to describe someone who committed the most serious type of offence. (The female version, 'Feloness' has rarely been used.) All capital offences, like murder and treason, were felonies but so also were theft and most offences against persons or property. Many carried the death penalty and medieval law had special ways of dealing with felons. In addition to the death penalty, felonies carried forfeiture of the felon's goods (see page 105) and new felonies were created by statute law well into the twentieth century.

Misdemeanours were less serious offences. They resulted from statutes or common law but did not carry forfeiture of property as a punishment—fines or imprisonment were used instead. But over the centuries the procedural differences between felonies and misdemeanours dwindled until there was very little true distinction. However, the difference remained vital to the policeman who had to arrest the offender. He could arrest, without a warrant, anyone who committed a felony within his view, or whom he reasonably suspected to have committed a felony. He could also arrest on the charge of a reliable third person. Felonies included murder and treason, but also a bewildering variety of crimes like robbery, manslaughter, rape, wounding, assault with intent to rob, attempted murder, causing injury by explosives, burglary, housebreaking, larceny, embezzlement, arson, piracy, making counterfeit coins, forgery, malicious damage and many others.

So far as misdemeanours were concerned, a policeman could arrest only if the offender committed the offence in his presence, and if a breach of the peace was committed. There are often statutory powers to arrest offenders but even so the distinction between felonies and misdemeanours did give rise to concern. It ended on 1 January 1968 when the Criminal Law Act 1967 came into force. The distinction between felonies and misdemeanours was abolished and a new name was created for criminal offences: an 'arrestable offence'. At the same time, new powers were given to arrest, to use force, and to search. An arrestable offence is as follows:

(i) Any offence for which the penalty is fixed by law. This includes murder, for example, where the penalty is fixed at life imprisonment
(ii) Any offence carrying imprisonment for five years or more on first conviction
(iii) Any attempt to commit offences at (i) and (ii) above.

The offence of taking a conveyance without the owner's consent as defined in the Theft Act 1968 is deemed to be an arrestable offence, although it only carries three years imprisonment. This is the only exception to the rules given above. There are many other offences, of course, for which statutes have given a specific power of arrest, such as those contained in the Firearms Act 1968, the Children and Young Persons Act 1933 and others. When creating the new classification, the Criminal Law Act went on to give the police *and the public* very wide powers to arrest offenders and to use force. In many ways this Act replaced common law on the subject.

The reform has affected all manner of legal process. It will for example, affect a strange society which still exists in the writer's home village, namely, the Glaisdale & Lealholm Association for the Prosecution of Felons, a voluntary law-enforcement organisation which has existed since the Middle Ages. This type of group was common in the eighteenth century when villagers formed themselves into associations to assist the parish constable to control crime. They built up their finances from rewards for retrieved cattle, etc, and although the Glaisdale & Lealholm Association has acquired fringe benefits such as a funeral club, expenses for jury service, etc, its prime duty is still the prosecution of felons. This association is thought to be the only one left in England and its members' only function now is to enjoy the annual dinner. As felons have disappeared, one wonders about the future of this unique relic of medieval law. It is such anachronisms, and the ancient courts which still persist, that make English law so interesting. The old mixes with the new in a most remarkable way. English law has a reputation for resisting change, and yet there has always been a high degree of flexibility within the system. The latest suggested reforms were published in September 1969 in the *Report of the Royal Commission on Assizes and Quarter Sessions 1966–69*. This recommends the abolition of assizes and quarter sessions, both cornerstones of the English legal system, and it is suggested they be replaced by crown courts which would be the only criminal courts above magistrates' court level and which would be based on the crown courts of Liverpool and Manchester. The report also made recommendations for the civil courts; these are incorporated in the text of this book as are the report's recommendations for certain ancient and curious courts. The latest change occurred in December 1969 when both Houses of Parliament voted for the abolition of the death penalty for murder.

TWO
The High Courts

THE HOUSE OF LORDS

The House of Lords, known as the High Court of Parliament, is the highest court in the realm. It has both appellate and original jurisdiction although at a court of first instance (ie the trying of a case without such case passing through any previous court) it is, in practice, nowadays seldom used.

Its role as a court has a long history which can perhaps be traced to pre-Conquest times when the sovereign was assisted in the government of his country by his Great Council, or Witan. The functions of this council were mainly advisory and the gathering was sometimes called the Assembly of the Wise; Magna Carta called it the Common Counsel of our Realm. Among its members were several judges, as well as bishops, archbishops and noblemen. When completely assembled, the Witan was occasionally asked to settle legal problems. Members who were not judges took part in making such decisions. As a result, the Witan was a combined advisory council and law court; it was also an exchequer (see page 181).

In 1265, Simon de Montfort instructed provincial knights to attend meetings of the Council and this can be regarded as the beginnings of Parliament. His action was ratified thirty years later in 1295 when Edward I said that representatives from all provincial towns and counties must attend. From this came the formation of the earliest House of Lords when, in 1305, Edward sent home all members of the Council except the bishops, counts, barons, justices and others who were also members of the Great Council. These formed a select gathering whose job was to discuss matters of great importance, but

17

even so these people met in the same room as the fully constituted Council. They had no separate building until 1342.

The real break between Parliament and the Great Council
occurred during the reign of Richard II (1377-99) when the
Great Council was sometimes called the Lords' House of Parliament. Even at that time, the latter dealt with appeals from
the King's Bench courts; errors by the courts were amended in
the lower Parliament. The birth of the present House of Lords
and its jurisdiction as a court is already evident. Precisely
when the Great Council actually became the House of Lords
is difficult to ascertain, but in the fourteenth century the House
of Lords was regarded as the highest judicial court in the land.
During the reign of Edward IV (1461-83) the assent of both
Houses was necessary before an Act became law, and this
ruling still remains.

As a court of first instance, some of the House of Lords'
first cases were trials of its own members who had committed
treasons and felonies. It had long been customary in England
that a peer of the realm who committed these offences had to
be tried by his equals and this was effective until 1948. The
custom included the wife or widow (until remarriage) of a
peer. The last trial of a peer by his peers occurred in 1936
when Lord de Clifford was committed on a coroner's warrant
for manslaughter as the result of a motoring accident. He was
found not guilty by eighty-five other peers. Four King's Bench
judges attended although there were five lords in the House
who held high judicial office. This ruling only applied to
felonies and treasons; misdemeanours committed by peers
could be tried by the magistrates or any criminal court,
although an Elizabethan statute said that if a peer committed
the misdemeanour of disturbing public worship after two previous convictions, he had to be tried by his peers.

The House of Lords has occasionally tried persons who were
not peers. In 1387, for example, it tried the Archbishop of
York, some peers and commoners for treason. Its last case as
a court of first instance came in the 1660s with a civil claim
for damages between a man called Skinner and the East India
Company. The case created trouble between both Houses, and

the Lords never again acted as a court of first instance in civil matters, except in cases of privilege. When the Criminal Justice Act of 1948 abolished the trial of a peer by his peers for felony and treason, its original jurisdiction in criminal matters was limited to impeachment. In other words, its original jurisdiction is practically obsolete, although this still remains in peerage claims, ie to the title to a peerage.

The Lords' function as a court is therefore currently to hear appeals from civil and criminal process. In the nineteenth century, though, there was a move to abolish these functions. This arose through the growth of the appeal courts (chapter six) which, it was felt, could perform all necessary appeal duties without recourse to the House of Lords. But apart from hearing English appeals, the Lords serves as the final appeal court for Wales; it also hears appeals from Scotland and Northern Ireland whose judicial systems are distinct from those of England and Wales. Records show that in the nineteenth century it dealt primarily with Scottish cases for the reason that, according to Scottish law, any such appeal gave an automatic stay of execution. It was logical that the Scots would appeal, and because of this the English judiciary could hardly abolish the appellate jurisdiction of the Lords.

Various committees were established by the government during the nineteenth century in an effort to solve these problems. In each case their function was to examine the appeals system with special emphasis on the role of the House of Lords. There were many difficulties—one of them was that so few of its members held legal qualifications, although it was required to sit as a court. This anomaly led to a demand for a professional judiciary in the House of Lords; this was vital if it was to continue as High Court of Parliament. The fact that most of its members were lay peers was recognised by the House itself, and the last time a lay peer voted in a judicial hearing was in 1834. By 1844, it was an accepted practice that lay peers did not vote on legal matters but, clearly, if the lay peers were not permitted to vote, the House of Lords must have some legally qualified members.

In 1856 an effort at solution was made by attempting to

grant peerages to certain judges but this did not meet with approval. By the 1860s, however, the House did have a reasonable number of legally qualified members because several Lord Chancellors became superfluous through rapid changes in administration. They were peers, they held legal qualifications, and so they remained in the Lords as 'peers who had held·high judicial office'. The role of the Lord Chancellor is explained later.

Over this period—the mid-nineteenth century—there was a far-reaching reform of the courts which included the appeals system. In 1869, the Royal Commission on the Judicature recommended the establishment of one Supreme Court. It was to consist of a High Court and a Court of Appeal. Their recommendations, in Bill form, received royal assent on 7 August 1873 and were scheduled to become effective from November 1874. Due to political changes, however, the commencement date was delayed for twelve months and, after this, all further attempts to reintroduce the Bill met with failure. Nonetheless, the basic idea persisted and agreement over court reform was finally reached in the Supreme Court of Judicature Act 1875. In spite of all the other changes, the House of Lords remained as the final court of appeal and it retains this position today.

The Appellate Jurisdiction Act of 1876 declared this to be so and it also created the Law Lords. These were necessary to fill a gap and were chosen from the judges of the Supreme Court, or from legally qualified persons in England, Scotland and Ireland. They had to be barristers-at-law of a least fifteen years standing and were to be peers during their term of office. Any peers holding high judicial office, or who had held high judicial office, were likewise entitled to sit as Law Lords.

The position and jurisdiction of the House of Lords had now been statutorily recognised and today it is technically, in its entirety, a judicial body. In practice this is not so. There is no law to prevent peers with no legal knowledge or qualifications from voting on judicial questions, but, as already mentioned, none has sat in this capacity since 1844. Although this is an unwritten rule, it is obeyed automatically and no unqualified person ever sits to debate a judicial question.

For the exercise of its judicial functions, the House sits in two committees, the Committee of Privileges and the Appellate Committee. To hear an appeal, there must be present at least three of the following: the Lord Chancellor; the Lords of Appeal in Ordinary; peers who have held high judicial office. The Lord Chancellor, and ex-Lord Chancellors, are ex-officio members of the court. As the Lord Chancellor is a cabinet minister appointed by his prime minister, he leaves the post when the government is out of office; he then receives a peerage which qualifies him to sit in this court (ie he is a peer who has held high judicial office). The post of Lord Chancellor embraces legislative, executive and judicial powers. The Lords of Appeal in Ordinary are appointed by the Queen on the advice of the prime minister in consultation with the Lord Chancellor. Until 1958 they were life peers, but Lords appointed after the commencement of the Judicial Pensions Act 1959 will retire at seventy-five years of age. In order to qualify they must be barristers of at least fifteen years standing, or alternatively must have been a judge or Lord Justice for at least two years. There are, at the time of writing, ten Law Lords (whose correct title is Lords of Appeal in Ordinary), in addition to the ex-officio judges. Although to act as a court, the House of Lords must have a minimum of three judges, for practical purposes the number is usually five. An odd number is sought because their decisions are by a majority vote.

The House of Lords will hear appeals from the prosecution or the defence against decisions by criminal or civil divisions of the Court of Appeal, the Courts Martial Appeal Court and the Divisional Courts of Queen's Bench. Before an appeal can be heard by the Lords, however, it requires permission from the House of Lords itself, or from the Court of Appeal.

The Committee of Privileges is seldom called upon for its function is to decide whether or not old peerages can be revived. It may also decide the validity of new ones and claims are first made to the Crown, through the Home Secretary, from where they are sent to the Attorney General who reports to the Lords. The case is then heard by the Committee of Privileges.

Procedure

Appeals to the House of Lords must be based on points of law, although a question of fact may occasionally creep in. Well over half the applications to the Lords to hear an appeal are turned down.

A civil appeal must be lodged within three months of the judgement which gave rise to it and the petition for leave to appeal must be lodged within one month. This does not apply if leave has already been given by the Court of Appeal. The petitioner serves copies of his petition on the respondent and these must state the grounds for the appeal. Copies of these, plus the decision of the Court of Appeal, are lodged with the Judicial Office. Eventually, the parties appear before the Appeal Committee of the House of Lords which will decide whether the appellant can proceed. After notice of trial, the Lords will hear and determine the appeal.

So far as criminal appeals are concerned, appeal lies to the House of Lords only when the Court of Appeal (Criminal Division) has certified it involves a point of law of general public importance (see chapter six).

QUEEN'S BENCH DIVISION OF THE HIGH COURT
(King's Bench Division)

The title of Chief Justice of the King's Bench (*Capitalis justicarius ad placita coram Rege tenenda*) was a new title given to Robert de Brus on 8 March 1268. Hitherto the sole head of English justice had been the sovereign. By a statute of 1300 the King's Bench court was made moveable and in theory it travelled around the country, always with the king in attendance; but the royal presence was vital and because of this the the court was rarely held outside Westminster Hall. From 1649–60, when there was no king on the throne, the court was known as the Upper Bench, but at the restoration of the monarchy it regained its old title.

The unusual name of this court arises from a marble bench, 19ft long by 3ft wide, which was situated on the south-east side of Westminster Hall and was used by the justices when in session and by the medieval kings at their coronation feasts. It was known as the King's Bench, so that the room in question became known as the King's Bench court. The King's Bench Division included the Court of Exchequer and the Court of Common Pleas and they used this hall from the days of Magna Carta until the Royal Courts of Justice in the Strand, London, were opened by Queen Victoria in 1882. There were nineteen courts in this new building.

In the nineteenth century, England's judicial system underwent a massive reorganisation. After the Judicature Commission came the Judicature Act of 1873 by which, in 1875, the Queen's Bench Division, the Court of Exchequer and the Court of Common Pleas were amalgamated to reappear as one Supreme Court of Judicature. This was better known as the High Court of Justice. For a time, the new court operated at Westminster Hall where it was divided into five divisions. These were:

(i) Chancery Division
(ii) Queen's Bench (or King's Bench) Division
(iii) Common Pleas Division
(iv) Exchequer Division
(v) Probate, Divorce and Admiralty Division.

In 1880 an Order in Council abolished the offices of Chief Justice of Common Pleas and Chief Baron of Exchequer (iii and iv above). Their jurisdiction was incorporated in the Queen's Bench Division which functioned as a single court and from that time, the High Court had only three divisions:

(i) Chancery Division
(ii) Queen's Bench (or King's Bench) Division
(iii) Probate, Divorce and Admiralty Division.

Until the second merger in Victorian times, each court had

its own functions. Pleas of the Crown, however, were tried by Queen's Bench which also tried a few criminal cases not heard by the assizes or at the Old Bailey. Civil disputes were heard at the Court of Common Pleas whilst revenue cases came before the Court of Exchequer. These courts, however, were not too particular about their precise jurisdiction. It became common to deal with each other's cases, for no better reason than to gather fees for their respective officials. The merger in 1880 was therefore a logical step and the result is that the modern Queen's Bench Division has a very wide jurisdiction which includes some criminal cases. The title, of course, varies with the sex of the reigning monarch.

Two of its best-known criminal trials were both framed under the Treason Act of 1351: one in 1903 when Colonel Arthur Lynch was tried for High Treason and the other in 1916 when Sir Roger Casement appeared on a like charge. The defence arguments were similar in both cases, but Lynch was sentenced to death. His sentence was later commuted to life imprisonment and he was released after twelve months. Next he received a free pardon and eventually became a Member of Parliament. This is in odd contrast to Sir Roger Casement who was hanged on 3 August 1916.

Although Queen's Bench seldom exercises its criminal jurisdiction, it can do so in the following instances:

(i) Where any criminal information for a misdemeanour has been filed by the Attorney General. (If information is laid by the Attorney General, the jurisdiction can only be exercised by the Queen's Bench Division)

(ii) For any indictable offence in respect of which the High Court has directed that, in the interests of justice, the indictment be removed from the court where it would normally be tried.

Through its appellate jurisdiction, the Queen's Bench Division, sitting with two or more judges, can take an appeal in one of two forms, ie

(i) By an Order of Certiorari (and sometimes, but more rarely, by an Order of Prohibition or Mandamus). By this method, any proceedings by a court of quarter session or a lower court can be brought before Queen's Bench Division for review and, if necessary, quashed.

(ii) By way of Case Stated. Here the justices at a magistrates' court may be required by an appellant to state a case for the decision of Queen's Bench Division on a point of law which has arisen before them. This is applicable also to justices sitting at quarter sessions, but only on a matter arising on appeal from a magistrates' court.

Queen's Bench Division deals with the bulk of civil business in the High Court and is therefore very busy. In 1908, two temporary courts were added and are still used; in 1911 a new wing of eight courts was added. In 1966, six further courts were provided below the Great Hall. In addition eight make-shift courts were then in use and on 1 October 1968, HM Queen Elizabeth II opened yet another extension to the buildings in the Strand. This has provided a further twelve new courts, a massive library of 40,000 books and several new offices. Even so, a number of temporary courts are still in use.

Queen's Bench Division deals with most civil actions involving contract or tort. Those involving matters such as the construction of wills, mortgages, sales and purchase of land, etc, go to Chancery Division. Although Chancery can award damages, normally actions for damages are heard in the Queen's Bench Division.

An action begins by the service of a writ upon the defendant or his solicitor. Details of civil court procedure are given in chapter four.

THE CENTRAL CRIMINAL COURT
(The Old Bailey)

The Old Bailey was established by the Central Criminal Court Act of 1834 which made it a permanent court of assize

mediumgut, plake a poduniefska

for London and the suburbs. Today its administration and juris-
diction is governed by the Administration of Justice Act 1964.
The City of London quarter sessions are also held at the Old
Bailey.

It is perhaps the most familiar court building in the world,
standing as it does in the centre of London and surmounted by
its copper dome and 15ft high gilded statue of the figure of
Justice. One hand of the figure holds the traditional scales and
the other the famous sword of justice. This particular statue
is unique in that it is not symbolically blindfolded. Over the
door are carved the words 'Defend the children of the poor and
punish the wrongdoer'.

The site of the Old Bailey has a long criminal history. For
something in the region of a thousand years, persons have
been tried on this site, for this was the location of the in-
famous old Newgate prison. Centuries before that gaol was
built, an earlier one existed at the corner of Newgate Street,
at its junction with the street of the Old Bailey, and was one
of the gates of London, then a walled city, known as Newgate.
Those gates, apart from giving access to London, were also
prisons and guardrooms and, in addition, trials of prisoners
took place inside. Newgate is mentioned as a prison as early
as 1207, and was damaged in the Great Fire of 1666, but was
rebuilt.

Situated next to that ancient gaol was a building known as
the Justice House. This was alternatively called the Sessions
House and stood in the street called Old Bailey; it was built
in 1550. It was from this place that prisoners were taken to
and from Newgate prison along a passage called Birdcage Walk.
Deceased prisoners were buried in that passage.

The building acquired the nickname of Old Bailey in its
earliest days and this has been carried into modern legal history, although the court's official title is the Central Criminal
Court. Newgate prison stood until 1902; it was then demolished
to make room for the new Central Criminal Court. Although
this court had been established by law in 1834, the erection
of its buildings did not begin until the later date. The new
building was opened in February 1907 by King Edward VII

who said during the opening ceremony 'The barbarous penal code which was deemed necessary one hundred years ago, has been gradually replaced in the progress towards a higher civilisation, by laws breathing a more humane spirit and aiming at a nobler purpose'.

The Old Bailey is purely a criminal court. It has no civil jurisdiction nor does it hear appeals. It has, however, taken over part of the old Admiralty jurisdiction and consequently can deal with all offences committed on the high seas, such as piracy, plus those committed on inland waters and upon certain stretches of the major rivers. Generally speaking, it has the same criminal jurisdiction as an assize court, therefore, if a person commits an offence either in the city or county of London, in the county of Middlesex, or in the Metropolitan areas of Essex, Kent or Surrey, and if that offence is one which would normally be tried at an assize court, then its venue of trial will be the Old Bailey. It has all the powers of an assize court but unlike the assizes, does not belong to any circuit. Broadly speaking, its area of jurisdiction is Greater London. The procedure is similar to that of an assize court, or quarter sessions, and is therefore included in the section dealing with those courts (see page 33).

It must sit at least four times a year, but in fact sits twelve times. This means it is almost continually in session because of the tremendous number of cases which come before it. The dates of the sessions are fixed annually at a meeting of its judges. The jurisdiction of the Central Criminal Court may be exercised by any one or more of its judges; one judge is deemed to constitute the court which is a branch of the High Court.

In practice the Old Bailey is presided over by the recorder, the common serjeant and two judges from the Mayor's Court of the City of London. They are full-time judges and deal with most of the cases. Usually a Queen's Bench Division judge will attend on the second day of the sessions to try the more serious charges. Several ex-officio judges are entitled to sit. These include the Lord Mayor of London, Aldermen of the City of London, the Lord Chanceller, the Lord Chief Justice and judges of Queen's Bench Division. In addition, not more than six judges are appointed under the City of London (Courts) Act 1964 and there may be others at the discretion of the crown.

It is recommended by the *Royal Commission on Assizes and Quarter Sessions 1966–69* that the work and jurisdiction of the Old Bailey be absorbed into the proposed new crown courts.

THE CROWN COURTS OF LIVERPOOL AND MANCHESTER

In south Lancashire, the Crown Courts of Liverpool and Manchester are combinations of assizes and quarter sessions, in much the same way as is the Central Criminal Court. They sit every month under a full-time recorder who acts as judge. Grave criminal offences are still tried by the judges of assize on circuit, but the procedure in the crown courts is similar to that of assizes and quarter sessions (see page 33).

These courts grew from an inability to cope satisfactorily with the vast numbers of criminal cases in the Liverpool and Manchester area. In 1952, such cases occupied 215 days at the assizes and a committee was set up to seek a solution. In 1953, it recommended the formation of these two new courts to relieve the assizes by undertaking much of their work and in 1956, under the authority of the Administration of Justice Act of that year, they were opened.

The *Royal Commission on Assizes and Quarter Sessions 1966–69* recommended that the work and jurisdiction of these courts be absorbed into the proposed new crown courts which are broadly based on the Liverpool and Manchester courts.

THE ASSIZES

The whole of England and Wales, outside the London area, is divided into seven assize circuits and, at certain times of the year, judges of Queen's Bench Division of the High Court travel in the provinces to take assizes on these circuits. They deal with both civil and criminal matters and are somewhat remi-

niscent of the days of the General Eyre (see chapter eight).
The seven circuits are as follows:

Circuit	Area covered
South Eastern	East Anglia, the Home Counties and the South East Coast.
Western	Corresponds to the old Wessex area, from Hampshire to Cornwall.
Midland	Central and eastern Midlands.
Oxford	Parts of south and west Midlands and including Monmouthshire.
North Eastern	Yorkshire, Durham and Northumberland, which corresponds to the English portion of Northumbria. It includes York, with its own assizes, for this was a city of great historic and administrative importance.
Northern	Lancashire and the North West of England.
Wales & Chester	This is one circuit divided into two sections: north and south. Cheshire belongs to Wales but Monmouthshire (see above) belongs to the Oxford circuit.

There are one or two anomalies here. Oxford's importance arises due to its central position and also because it was a royalist capital during the civil wars. Birmingham is part of two circuits, ie Midland and Oxford.

The commissioners of assize hold a court in the assize town of each county, two, three or four times a year. Each circuit contains several towns which have assize courts; usually these towns have, or have had, a royal castle, the purpose of which was to provide suitable accommodation for both the visiting dignitaries and the prisoners awaiting trial. From this use of castles, and from the lack of assize courts in the new towns such as Teesside, it will be seen that our assize courts have a long history. It can, in fact, be traced to the very beginnings of our legal system and so the assizes epitomise the very essence of English law. It is in some respects sad that the *Royal Commission on Assizes and Quarter Sessions 1966–69* recommends their abolition.

The word 'assize' comes from the Latin *assideo* meaning 'I sit'. So far as legal process was concerned, it was used to indicate a periodic gathering of knights and other county men of similar standing, together with a bailiff or justice who sat to deal with matters of public interest. This was indeed a legacy of the days when the king, in person, visited his towns and cities to administer justice.

In 1166 the Assize of Clarendon ordered travelling justices to enquire into murder, robbery, larceny and the harbouring of criminals. It further decreed that persons suspected of those offences should appear before twelve men from each 'hundred' and four from each town. In 1176 this procedure was extended to include arson and forgery. This was perhaps the real beginning of the system for trying serious offences before a jury and was the forerunner of the assizes. The offences concerned were all felonies and involved forfeiture of the felon's goods to the Crown. Even a convict's land was forfeited to the king for a year and a day, after which time it was estreated to his lord. This did not apply in cases of treason, however, when the land went to the Crown for ever. Later all felonies except theft and petty mayhem were punishable by death; forgery was later reduced to a misdemeanour but, even so, many misdemeanours were dealt with by the travelling justices. The smaller courts—the county courts, hundred courts, manorial and borough courts—found their work drastically reduced although they did continue to deal with petty civil and criminal matters.

Oddly enough, many of the judges sent on circuit were not legally qualified. The professional judges remained at Westminster and those on circuit consisted of a strange collection of people—abbots, earls, chaplains, men of the king's household and even his closest friends. These men, who came from all walks of life, were predecessors of our modern judges of assize.

From these rather uncertain beginnings, grew our system of assize courts. The procedures which began centuries ago have changed very little; it was not until the nineteenth century that an accused person could give evidence on his own behalf. There have been blots, however; one of these took place in 1685 under Judge Jeffreys. He toured the West Country for trials after the Duke of Monmouth's unsuccessful rebellion and inflicted sentences of death, transportation and whipping with such severity that over 300 people were executed. His trials became known as the Bloody Assizes.

By and large, though, the assizes are the corner-stone of the English legal system and have wide powers and jurisdiction, both civil and criminal. With such historical beginnings, the opening of the assizes contains a great deal of ceremonial and pageantry, centred around the arrival of the robed judges at their courts. Other high officials and dignitaries, such as the sheriff, may be present at the assizes and may even sit in the court beside the judge. They take little or no part in the legal proceedings although they do have some administrative power.

An assize court judge represents the sovereign when in court, just as he did all those centuries ago, and it follows that he is a person of considerable importance. He is given a commission, in the form of letters patent, which instructs him to take the assizes on a named circuit. In overall charge of the circuits is the Lord Chief Justice. Assize judges are judges of the Queen's Bench Division and must receive adequate notice of these circuits to free themselves of other work over which assize courts always take precedence. When a judge receives his commission and is subsequently engaged in his work, he has all the power of a High Court judge—assizes are a branch of the High Court of Justice—and this gives them powers beyond their commission.

The commissions under which a judge sits are as follows:

(i) Assize	This confers upon him a civil jurisdiction.
(ii) Oyer and terminer	This means 'to hear and

	determine' and it gives him power to try all persons against whom an indictment has been presented within the circuit.
(iii) General gaol delivery	Under this commission all persons in prison or who have been released on bail, are tried.
(iv) The peace	This commission is given because every judge is a justice of the peace for every county.

At one time no judge or lawyer could act in the commission of oyer and terminer within the county where he was born or lived. This restriction was removed by George II in 1739.

Two or three judges often go on circuit together, although one of them is in charge of the entire commission. Occasionally as many as four may sit at one assizes in which case they share the work. Usually there are two judges—one to hear the criminal cases, the other to decide civil matters. If there is only one judge, he will deal with criminal matters first and, in any ceremonial, the criminal judge takes precedence over his civil assize colleague.

A criminal assize court does not hear appeals; it is concerned only with the trial of the more serious criminal offenders. Some offences such as murder, manslaughter, bigamy, criminal libel and treason can be dealt with only at an assize court; others, eg some forms of burglary, may be dealt with either at assizes, quarter sessions or even at a magistrates' court. Something like three-quarters of all indictable offences (ie those triable before a jury) are dealt with by quarter sessions. This leaves the assizes free to deal with the more serious matters. Assizes undertake a very small proportion of civil cases. Most of this type of business, because of its complexity, is done by the Queen's Bench Division in London.

On very rare occasions there is no crime list at a sitting of an assize court. When this happens the sheriff presents the judge with a pair of white kid gloves to commemorate the occasion. This is now known as a maiden assize, but until the mid-nineteenth century the name was given when no one was convicted of a capital offence.

PROCEDURE AT A CRIMINAL ASSIZE COURT
(including quarter sessions, the crown courts and the Old Bailey)

The procedure at assizes is akin to that of quarter sessions, the Old Bailey and the Crown Courts of Liverpool and Manchester, so all are included here. References to judge include chairman or recorder. Generally, a trial is held in public although a judge can order women and children to leave if he considers it necessary. He may also eject those who disturb the proceedings. A trial may be held in secret if national defence or official secrets are involved.

The first step in a trial is to call the defendant to the bar, which means he appears in the dock. He will have been sent to this court from the magistrates' court by what are known as committal proceedings (see page 66). During his trial, a prisoner is free from restraint unless he is violent and he will not be handcuffed or restricted in any way unless the judge feels it is necessary. When he is at the bar, the indictment will be read to him. If it contains several counts, each will be read separately and he will be asked to plead to each count as it is read.

Guilty plea

If a defendant pleads guilty, a trial is superfluous. In such a case the court will impose a sentence only, but prior to this the main facts of the charge will be considered, together with any statements made by the prisoner or his counsel. The antecedents will also be read to the court; this will include his previous character with convictions if any, a record of his employment, and his personal history. This enables a suitable punishment to be awarded. In practice, details of

c

convictions will always be supplied to the accused's defence counsel by the police so that he knows when he may safely put his client's character in issue.

When there is more than one accused, a plea of guilty by one must never be regarded as evidence against any other of the accused. Each must be separately tried. A defendant may plead guilty to some counts and not guilty to others, but all pleas of guilty must come from the prisoner himself, unless the defendant is a corporation (see page 36). They are not acceptable from anyone on his behalf, but a trial judge may refuse to accept guilty pleas when he considers a defendant unfit to plead. A person may be unfit to plead through insanity for example, and this will be decided by a jury empanelled for that purpose. If a guilty plea is not accepted, it will be regarded as withdrawn, so that the prisoner cannot be sentenced upon it if he is later acquitted by the jury. A plea of not guilty may, with the judge's consent, be withdrawn and changed to guilty. If this is done after the prisoner is in the charge of the jury (ie when the trial has started) the jury must give a verdict. If this is not done, the trial is null and void.

Pleas which are neither guilty nor not guilty

Motion to quash indictment. This is made on the grounds of some irregularity or invalidity, but if the defect was of a minor nature the motion would be made before the plea. This makes it possible for the court to remedy the defect.

When the defect is substantial, the motion must be made after the plea has been taken. If the motion was shown to be of substance, the indictment would be quashed. In the event of doubt, the court will not quash the indictment but the accused would have the opportunity of proceeding by demurrer.

Demurrer. This is an objection through which an accused can admit the facts which form the charge, but claim they do not amount to an offence in law. He may alternatively claim they do not amount to the offence with which he is charged. This form of objection is made before the plea, but the court may withdraw a plea so that a defendant can demur. A demurrer must be made in writing, and the prisoner can, since the Criminal Law Act 1967, enter a plea of not guilty as well as a demurrer.

Plea to the jurisdiction. This is used when a person appears before a court and is charged with an offence over which that particular court has no jurisdiction. In this instance he can plead to the jurisdiction without answering the charge. This is a very rare type of plea because the usual course would be to proceed by a motion to quash the indictment. In the event of a conviction by a court having no jurisdiction, an accused could lodge an appeal. A plea to the jurisdiction must be in writing.

Special pleas in bar. These are rare but the following come under this heading:

(i) *Autrefois acquit and autrefois convict.* The maxim here is that no man shall be twice put in peril for the same offence. These pleas are put forward on the grounds that a man has already been tried for the offence and has either been acquitted or convicted.

(ii) *Pardon.* The Royal Pardon may be pleaded in the bar to the indictment; or after the verdict, in arrest of judgement; or after judgement in bar of execution. If a defendant does not put forward this plea at the earliest oportunity, he will be deemed to have waived benefit of it.

Unfit to stand trial. A person suffering from mental disorders, or who is incapable of understanding the proceedings, may not be fit to stand trial. The question is usually decided by a jury other than that which is to try the case, and it is done at the trial. In exceptional cases, however, the Home Secretary may order the person's removal to hospital, prior to the trial. To do this, he must see reports from two registered medical practitioners to the effect that the person is suffering from mental illness or severe subnormality to a degree that warrants his detention in a hospital.

In cases where a court finds a person is unfit to plead, the trial will not continue and the court will make an order admitting the accused to a hospital nominated by the Secretary of State. An appeal against a finding of unfitness to plead lies to the Court of Appeal.

Not guilty plea

'Plead to the general issue' is the technical way of pleading not guilty, because when a person speaks these words he is deemed to have put himself upon the country for trial. The prosecutor must prove beyond all reasonable doubt every fact which constitutes the offence charged, whilst the defendant should prove all the facts which rebut the prosecution's case.

If a prisoner declines to plead, a plea of not guilty is entered. A corporation can plead guilty or not guilty through a representative but if this person fails to appear, or does not put forward his plea, the court shall enter a plea of not guilty.

Once a defendant has pleaded not guilty, he is handed over to the jury and the procedure thereafter is outlined in the following pages.

THE JURY

Early traces of a jury system are to be found in the oath-helpers, known as compurgators, who existed in Anglo-Saxon times. It is on record that in 866-71, the laws of Ethelred provided that twelve freeholders of each 'hundred' should swear to accuse no innocent person or conceal guilty ones, but apart from these factual snippets, the precise origins of the jury are uncertain. It may have been introduced to England by the Normans in the eleventh century although, under the Danes, land disputes were settled by a sworn verdict of a group of local people.

At the Assize of Clarendon in 1166, however, Henry II established a definite form of jury. It was alternatively known as a grand jury or a jury of presentment, and its job was to bring local criminals before the king's justices for trial. It also served on inquests. The notion behind a grand jury was that it was a representative body which could accuse persons too powerful for a single person to confront. This was felt necessary for a fair judicial system. Henry II also instituted petty juries in the royal courts as an alternative to the old-fashioned trials by ordeal, water or battle. As these forms of justice disappeared, jurors were regularly used. All this took time: Henry II who originated the system, did not live to see trial by jury as we know it and in those early days the jurors were prosecutors rather than deciders. The outcome of a case depended upon their own personal knowledge of the person on trial and his deeds, but as the Middle Ages began to produce a more sophisticated legal system it was realised that such jurors could not by themselves be relied upon to decide fairly a person's guilt or innocence.

It was during these formative stages that judges began to admit other witnesses at their trials. These were not part of the jury and attended to give independent evidence. This became routine procedure and today the system is firmly established although it is governed by a host of rules which regulate the progress of a case. The rules are known as the Rules, or Laws, of Evidence and apply to civil and criminal cases.

From this early but important distinction between witnesses and jurors the foundations of the modern jury were established. But the difficulty still existed that the jurors knew all about the case they had to try. They knew the accused and his personal history, and it must have been a most difficult, if not impossible, task to produce a truly impartial verdict. Oddly enough, it was not until the eighteenth century that persons were barred from acting as jurors if they had any previous knowledge of a case. Today, this is regarded as vital; impartiality is the keystone of the jury system. The jury has the effect of putting the man-in-the-street into the law courts to see fair play.

Selection of jurors

Jurors possess no legal qualifications and are drawn from people doing ordinary jobs. Even so, there are rules which govern their selection, although until the advent of the Criminal Justice Act 1967 there appeared to be a certain laxity in this respect.

To be selected as a juror, a person must have several qualifications. At the time of writing, one is property ownership. This qualification has existed almost since the earliest juries whose members were appointed locally, by, for example, the parish constable. Selection was influenced by the local aristocracy who regarded the visit of an assize judge as a major social event. Because of the snobbery involved, persons of high social standing obtained seats on the juries in the assize courts while the minor juries at quarter sessions were staffed by farmers and tradesmen.

To avoid possible favouritism in this method of selection the Juries Act of 1825 standardised procedure. It retained the holding of land as a qualification and is still in force. It says that a person is liable for jury service if he occupies a dwelling with a rateable value of £20 (apart from London and Middlesex where the figure is £30). It also makes liable, persons who own freehold land with an annual value of at least £10, or a person with a tenancy of twenty-one years or more having an annual value of at least £20, or even a person who occupies a house with at least fifteen windows! These rules did not apply to the selection of city and borough jurors. They followed their own procedure until 1922, and it did not affect coroners' juries (see page 115).

Today, through the decrease in the value of money, many persons qualify for jury membership merely by reason of the place in which they live and this has created problems. For example, people of the lower criminal classes now qualify and yet the Act rules out many ideal women. This and other relevant problems were discussed by the Home Office and, in 1965, a committee considered the proper qualifications of a juror. This committee, under Lord Morris, made suggestions which were included in the Criminal Justice Act of 1967 which sought to modernise legal procedure. This Act mainly became operative on 1 January 1968 and its provisions are included later (see pages 39 and 44).

In 1825, the upper age limit for jurors was fixed at 60 years, although for the duration of the two World Wars this was increased to 65 as a temporary measure. The lower qualifying age remains at 21 because the reduction of the voting age to 18 on 1 January 1970 does not mean that such youngsters can sit on a jury even if they have the other necessary qualifications, such as property ownership. Few persons aged 21 have the necessary property qualifications and so most juries consist of members in early or late middle age. That a person is listed for jury service is indicated by a letter J against his name in the electoral register for his locality. This can be inspected in the post office.

Before 1949 there were two types of jury, ie common and special. Special juries appear to have operated since the thirteenth century when they consisted of persons with a professional knowledge of the subject under trial. For example, a mercantile dispute would be settled by a jury of tradesmen who had knowledge of the trade in question and in some of the higher courts, such as King's Bench Division, it became a regular practice to empanel jurors who were of high status. In King's Bench Division it was decided in 1730 that a special jury could be requested for a fee in both civil and criminal cases which came before it.

The 1825 Act said that special jurors should be bankers, merchants, or esquires and to this was added in 1870 a property qualification such as applied to common juries—the rateable value was proportionately higher. Special juries were of little or no value in a criminal trial and in the early part of the twentieth century the principle was felt to be wrong, even in civil disputes. As a result, special juries were abolished in 1949 with the exception of those in the commercial courts of Queen's Bench Division. Even so, no special jury seems to have sat since 1950.

With the inception of the Criminal Justice Act 1967 certain convicted persons cannot sit on a jury. Before this Act, it was usual for the police to examine the lists of forthcoming jury members with a view to the removal of convicted nominees. This savoured of police collusion in jury selection but today the law bans such persons as follows:

    (i) Any person who has served any part of a three-month prison sentence (including borstal or detention during HM pleasure) is barred for ten years after his release.

    (ii) Any person sentenced to life imprisonment, or who has served any part of a sentence of imprisonment of at least five years is disqualified for life.

These disqualifications apply even if the letter J appears against such a person's name in the electoral register. If such a person does sit on a jury which delivers a verdict before he is discovered, his presence does not invalidate that verdict. If he is found before the verdict, he will be removed. There are heavy penalties for convicted persons who sit on juries and a notice to this effect is given to jury members before they are sworn.

Aliens are excluded from jury service because they have no vote, but Commonwealth and Irish immigrants, including coloured persons, can serve once they are on the electoral register. They must, of course, possess the necessary property qualifications.

Various persons are exempt from jury service because of their work. These include: clergymen and nuns, county councillors, doctors, firemen, lawyers, members of Parliament, peers of the realm and police officers. There are many more exempted persons but professional people like teachers, businessmen and the like are not exempt even though attendance at court could interrupt their work.

When a person is named in the electoral roll as a possible juror, he will receive a notice in writing which allows him to object. He might have to apply to a magistrates' court for removal of his name, but any valid objection will be satisfactorily dealt with before this action is necessary. The task of selecting jurors, who may be male or female, lies with the summoning officer of each court and, by tradition, the sheriff of a county selects those for quarter sessions and assizes. Towns with their own borough quarter sessions employ a clerk of the peace who performs this task. He is often the town clerk or some other local government official.

Juries will always be found in the superior courts, ie the assizes, the Central Criminal Court and the crown courts. They are also found in quarter sessions, but never in magistrates' courts. They are comparatively rare in civil courts although they are used in a few High Court cases and on very rare occasions in the county courts. Juries are also found in coroners' courts, some tribunals and at the quaint, but annual, Trial of the Pyx. The selection of these latter juries is not bound by the rules governing those in the higher courts.

Empanelling a jury

At the appropriate time, a summons will be sent to the nominated persons and there will be enough persons called to allow for excuses through valid reasons. It is the duty of the summoning officer to make sure there are sufficient jurors for each session. When a person is summoned for jury service, it is open for him to give a good reason why he should not attend. The obvious ones include illness, or running a one-man business, and every application for release will be dealt with on its merits. The mere fact of serving on a jury may excuse a person from further service over a stated period. In any case no juror may serve more than once in a year, but a judge can excuse a juror from further service either for life, or for a long period, and this power is occasionally exercised after a jury has sat for a long time in a difficult case.

The persons summoned as jurors will attend the court at the time and date given in their summons and they are collectively known as a panel of jurors. Each separate panel of twelve will be selected by ballot from the assembled numbers and at the appropriate time they will be shown into the jury box. A judge may order a jury to consist entirely of men or of women, but usually it is mixed. Each member will enter the box when his name is called and their collective duty is to try defendants who have pleaded not guilty—those pleading guilty will have been sentenced without the need of a jury to determine their guilt.

When the twelve jurors are assembled in their seats, the prisoner will be told that he may, without giving a reason, challenge any individual member. There are two types of challenge, each used in particular circumstances:

(i) The peremptory challenge, which is the one showing no cause
(ii) A challenge for cause, for which some definite reason must be stated and proved.

Seven peremptory challenges can be made by the defence but the prosecution does not possess this right. It can, however, request a juror, or even several jurors, to 'stand by' without reason. Challenges for cause can be made by either the prosecution or the defence and fall into two types:

(i) A challenge to the array
(ii) A challenge to the polls.

A challenge to the array means a challenge to the jury as a whole. It can be made on the grounds of the sheriff's partiality and should be made in writing, stating the reasons for the objection, before any of the jurors are sworn. The sheriff, it will be remembered, selected the jury from qualified persons. A challenge to the polls, on the other hand, is one to individual jurors and can be made after an unsuccessful challenge to the array. It can, in cases of treason for example, be made by a defendant who has used all his permitted peremptory challenges. A challenge to the polls is an oral challenge.

The prisoner is told of his right to challenge any of his jurors by being addressed by the clerk of the court in the following way:

Prisoner at the bar. The names that you are about to hear called are the names of the jurors who are to pass between our Sovereign Lady the Queen [or Sovereign Lord the King] and yourself upon your trial. If therefore you wish to object to them or to any of them, you must do so as they come to the book to be sworn, and before they are sworn, and your objection shall be heard.

The challenge is made by calling out the word 'challenge' as the juror in question comes to be sworn. Any doubt as to the validity of a challenge for cause will be determined by the court.

A challenge is a comparative rarity, but even rarer is an insufficiency of jurors for a trial, due to the challenges in court, or some other reason. In such a case, the judge may command that numbers be made up from persons within the precincts of the court. This is an ancient procedure called 'praying a tales' (pronounced taylees). The word comes from the Latin *tales de circumstandibus* which means 'from such persons who are standing about'. It is not permitted to empanel an entire jury by this rather harsh method and such talesmen must be in addition to those jurors already summoned. The custom is used only in cases of extreme emergency.

Once the jury is over the challenge stage, each member is individually sworn by taking an oath that he will faithfully try the case and give a true verdict according to the evidence. The prisoner is formally handed over to the jury by the clerk of the court who says:

Members of the jury. The prisoner stands indicted for that he on the . . . [date and details of the charge]. To this indictment he has pleaded not guilty and it is your charge to say, having heard the evidence whether he is guilty or not.

The trial then begins. During the hearing, the jury must listen to the evidence and inspect exhibits produced.

At the trial

The prosecution will open the case and will produce witnesses who will tell the court of what they saw or heard. Each takes the oath before beginning and is examined on his evidence by the prosecuting counsel. This is the examination-in-chief, after which each witness is cross-examined by the defending counsel. Then, if necessary, the witness will be re-examined by the prosecution. When all the prosecution witnesses have been heard the defence may submit that there is no case to answer; if this is upheld the prisoner will be discharged. If not, the trial will continue by the production of the defence witnesses and the same procedure applies. Each will be examined, cross-examined and re-examined on his evidence until all have been heard. The jury must listen to the evidence for it is upon this, and this alone, that they must form their verdict.

After all the evidence has been presented, each side will address the court and emphasise its own aspect of the case by pinpointing the opposition's weaknesses. It is an established rule that the prosecution must address the jury before the defence has the final word. The judge will then sum up, directing the jury on points of law and generally condensing the trial evidence for their benefit.

The jury will then consider its verdict, almost invariably by retiring to a nearby room to discuss it. They will appoint among themselves a foreman, and must remain together once they have begun discussions. If a point arises where they need help, they may return to the court to ask assistance from the judge, but this discussion will be heard by the defending counsel. They will then continue their secret deliberations and may have reasonable refreshment if it takes a long time.

A jury must strive towards a unanimous verdict and, until 31 December 1967, only a unanimous one was acceptable. With effect from 1 January 1968, however, the Criminal Justice Act introduced majority verdicts which are now accepted by the courts on certain occasions. To qualify for a majority verdict, a jury must deliberate for at least two hours, or for such longer time thought fit by the judge. If after this time they cannot agree, then a majority verdict may be given.

For a full jury of 12, a majority vote of at least 10 to 2 is acceptable; if the jury consists of 11 persons the valid majority is 9 to 2, and for a 10-man jury, it is 9 to 1. The absolute minimum to constitute a jury is 9 members and if, through illness or other reasons, a jury is reduced to 9, then all 9 must give a unanimous decision. They cannot give a majority verdict.

If the majority verdict is one of guilty, the foreman must inform the court that it was a majority verdict, and furthermore he must state the numbers for and against the decision. Failure to do this would invalidate the decision. In the event of a not guilty verdict, however, it is not necessary to state the numbers for and against, nor even to say it was a majority verdict. This is to prevent a person found not guilty by such a verdict being harassed if it became known that some of the jury felt he was guilty.

The introduction of the majority verdict system was partly to speed the processes of justice, but mainly to exclude or diminish the possibility of false decisions through bribery or other pressures on the jury members. One of the longest times taken to deliver a verdict occurred during the trial of the Great Train Robbers of 1963 when the jury deliberated for sixty-seven hours. This was before the introduction of majority verdicts.

When a jury returns a verdict of guilty, whether by majority vote or not, the prisoner will be sentenced by the judge for his crime. Any previous convictions will first be read to the court and the jury have no say in the awarding of the punishment. If the verdict is not guilty, the prisoner will be discharged and is free to leave the court. Always, the jury is thanked by the judge for their services and discharged.

THREE
Magistrates And Their Courts

MAGISTRATES

It is difficult to trace the precise origins of the justice of the peace, or magistrate as he is otherwise known. This office has played a major role in the development of the law and has a splendid history. Today the magistrates (men and women) have courts of their own—the quarter sessions and the magistrates' courts—each dealt with in this chapter.

It is possible that Archbishop Hubert in the late twelfth century, appointed knights to help keep order. Some legal historians believe that he founded the office of justice, but in 1264 Simon de Montfort appointed men known as keepers of the peace (*custodes pacis*). These men, who were appointed in every county, were really soldiers who served until the king and his barons decided otherwise. Their duties gradually changed until they were mainly civil rather than military and by the fourteenth century this process was complete. The title of justice of the peace first appears in 1362.

In 1316, before the appearance of this name, these officials were given the power to arrest offenders and suspects. They could also enquire into felonies and trespasses. It took less than a dozen years for them to be accepted as part of English life. In 1327, some members of Parliament wanted them to *punish* offenders and, although this power was not granted at that stage, Parliament did empower them to do this only two years later. But this did not last—the power was revoked in the following year and then came a see-saw of decisions until 1332 when their powers to punish were once more restored. By this time they could detain suspects until the arrival of the royal justices and could issue warrants for arrest.

Their value as law enforcement officers, albeit secondary to the royal justices, could not be doubted. They fell between these important justices on the one hand and the work of the local and manorial courts on the other. During medieval times their powers and functions multiplied and strengthened and after 1345 they were empowered to try offenders at quarter sessions. This gave them a very wide and powerful jurisdiction, but their powers decreased as some duties were taken over by the higher courts. Even so, the justices were an essential part of English law and were given administrative powers in their role of keepers of the king's peace. In the latter part of the fourteenth century, they had to supervise prices and wages and were given similar tasks which seemed far from their primary duty. It was not until the formation of the county councils in the nineteenth century that many ancient powers were removed from the justices and allocated elsewhere.

The method of appointment of a justice has varied over the centuries. As early as 1388 it was the responsibility of the Lord Chancellor and other royal officials. Henry V decided that the chancellor's role should be merely advisory and, by the time Henry VIII came to the throne, these appointments were the entire responsibility of the Crown, although the Lord Chancellor always gave advice. From the eighteenth century he was assisted by the Lord Lieutenant of the respective county and this system exists today. In practice, the Lord Chancellor is responsible for the appointment of magistrates although they are nominally Crown appointments. Within the Duchy of Lancaster the chancellor of the duchy appoints his magistrates instead of the Lord Chancellor.

At the outset, a magistrate was paid a few shillings per day, but it quickly ceased to be a paid office and, by the end of the seventeenth century, the only perk was an annual free dinner. Today only expenses are allowed; there is no salary.

The Justices Qualification Act of 1774 enacted that, to qualify as a justice, a candidate must have an estate with an annual value of £100. A year later this was altered to occupancy of a house rated at £100. Before this Act, land-owners, including some women, became justices—ownership of property has been a traditional qualification for several legal offices, jurors and coroners for example. In 1906 the property qualification for justices was abolished and they could live up to seven miles from their county. Since 1949 the residential qualification has been within fifteen miles of their respective commission of the peace. This does not apply to stipendiary magistrates (see page 50). Women have been statutorily eligible for appointment to the bench since 1919. Boroughs (other than the very small ones) generally have their own commissions of the peace.

There are approximately 16,000 magistrates in the country with an annual intake of roughly 1,000. Magistrates leave the bench for various reasons such as old age or ill-health, and they have to be replaced. Over and above this, the Lord Chancellor can remove them for misbehaviour. This means that there is a constant turnover of magistrates.

There is a supplemental list of magistrates, sometimes known as the retired list, and those who reach retiring age are placed upon it. A magistrate must step down from the bench when he reaches retirement age but, by being on the list, he can remain a magistrate and, although he cannot sit in court, he can still perform smaller tasks such as witnessing signatures. A magistrate may also be put on this list if he does not fulfil the residential qualification, ie if he moves house more than the permitted fifteen miles from his county or borough and so ceases to qualify for his original area. He may therefore be on the list as a temporary measure and may eventually be appointed to a bench in his new area. The names are put on the list by either the town clerk or the clerk of the peace or perhaps by someone else holding the commission of the peace. A person may apply to be placed on the list but this must have the consent of the Lord Chancellor. The latter may also order magistrates to be put on the list for health reasons or even through failure to carry out their duties. Some ex-officio justices may be placed on the list for like reasons.

Until the Justice of the Peace Act 1968, a magistrate's retiring age (including City of London aldermen) was 75. With the passing of this Act it was reduced to 70 but, to prevent a sudden over-depletion of numbers, the age reduction will extend over the five years 1969-73. The age limit will therefore reduce one year at a time. A magistrate who is chairman or deputy chairman of quarter sessions, or who is a recorder, or who holds or has held high judicial office, is exempt from this provision. High Court judges, for example, retire at 75.

A person cannot act as a justice if he has any interest, pecuniary or otherwise, which might lead to a miscarriage of justice in any proceedings. Nonetheless, if such interest is known to all parties, objections may be waived and subsequent proceedings will not be invalid. An example of this might occur when a justice tries a case involving a relation or an employee.

Other persons forbidden to act as magistrates include a justice who is a member of a local authority—he cannot sit at proceedings for or against the authority concerned. Similarly when proceedings are taken under the Hosiery Act 1843 at least one of the magistrates must not be engaged in that trade. This type of rule applies to laws which govern the trade unions. Generally a person's profession will not prevent him from being a magistrate because ideally all trades, professions and classes should be represented on the bench. Some persons, however, cannot be elected because of their profession. The sheriff of a county cannot be a justice for that county, neither can a magistrates' clerk, should he be appointed to the bench.

Crimes of a serious nature naturally prevent anyone convicted of them from acting as a magistrate. If a magistrate is convicted of treason or a serious offence for which he is sentenced to death or to imprisonment for more than twelve months, or if he is convicted of corrupt practice at a parliamentary or municipal election, then this will lead to his removal from office.

On the civil side, no bankrupt person can be appointed and this applies equally to ex-officio justices. When a bankrupt is discharged, however, he may return to the office if he has a

D

certificate to show that his bankruptcy was due to mistakes and not to misconduct.

As well as judicial work, magistrates also act in an administrative capacity, granting licences to bookmakers, betting operators, public house licensees, gaming personnel and others. They also have a limited jurisdiction over civil and domestic matters. Due to modern training, benches are increasingly efficient in their work. From 1 January 1966, a new justice has had to go for a short training course and there is a special course for those who serve in juvenile courts.

Stipendiary magistrates

Stipendiary magistrates date from the eighteenth century and were originally to be found only in London. They were used in lieu of the poor quality lay magistrates of that time and were in charge of the constables until 1839. After that time a commissioner became responsible for the police of the metropolis and today the Commissioner of the Metropolitan Police is still a magistrate, a relic of those days. It was in 1792 that several paid magistrates were first appointed and in 1813 a stipendiary magistrate was permitted in Manchester. During the nineteenth century, boroughs and certain other areas were granted powers to ask for stipendiary magistrates. Today a county or a borough may petition for a stipendiary magistrate who is appointed by the Crown on advice from the Lord Chancellor. There can be no new appointment unless a borough makes the necessary request.

A stipendiary magistrate must be a barrister or a solicitor of at least seven years standing and he differs from a lay magistrate in that he is paid a salary. This is fixed by the Lord Chancellor and is paid by the respective local authority.

If a stipendiary magistrate retires or dies there must be a request for a successor and it was not until recently that there was a retiring age, or even a pension, for these officials. The Justice of the Peace Act 1949 put matters right and established a retiring age of 72. This was reduced to 70 in 1969.

These magistrates are usually found in towns with over 25,000 population. In the Inner London area, there are Metropolitan stipendiary magistrates who are appointed from practising lawyers and who do not exceed forty in number. One of them is appointed by the Lord Chancellor to be Chief Magistrate. Metropolitan stipendiary magistrates always sit alone for summary cases and do not have a jury. In the provinces, however, their colleagues may sit on a bench consisting of lay magistrates in which case they act as chairman. When sitting alone, a stipendiary magistrate has the power of a bench. There are very few stipendiary magistrates outside London.

Ex-officio magistrates

Until 1969, roughly 2,000 persons qualified as ex-officio magistrates due merely to their official position. Some of them rarely acted in this capacity, although many did sit on the magisterial bench. Most of them are now disqualified.

The following were ex-officio magistrates for *every* county :

* The Lord Chancellor
* The Lord President of the Council
* The Lord Privy Seal and members of the Privy Council
* The Lord Chief Justice
* The Master of the Rolls
* The Lord Justices of Appeal
* Judges of the High Court
* The Attorney General
* The Solicitor General

In addition each county had its own particular ex-officio justices which included :

* The chairman of the county council
* The chairman of the UDC or RDC
* Mayors of boroughs not holding their own commission of the peace
* The chief magistrate at Bow Street

In particular boroughs, the following held office as ex-officio magistrates :

52   THE COURTS OF LAW
    * The mayor
    The recorder
    The judge of the county court in London
    A stipendiary magistrate
    The commissioner and assistant commissioner of the Metropolitan police
    Legally qualified chairmen of the county quarter sessions

Other ex-officio magistrates included ecclesiastical and university dignitaries.

Of those ex-officio magistrates who still remain, the chairman of the Greater London Council is a justice for each of the London commission areas and the chief magistrate of the Metropolitan Police Court at Bow Street becomes a magistrate for Berkshire when his name is inserted in the commission of that county. He does not take any oath of qualification.

For boroughs with their own commissions of the peace, the judge of the county court may be included in the commission of the county or borough where the court is situated. Similarly a stipendiary magistrate is an ex-officio justice for any county or borough which includes his area. Furthermore, both the commissioner and assistant commissioner of the Metropolitan police are justices for the counties of Surrey, Essex, Hertfordshire, Kent, Berkshire and Buckinghamshire, and for each of the London commission areas, although they do not act as magistrates at a judicial hearing. Their counterpart in the City of London, the commissioner of the City of London police, may be a magistrate for the City, and the chairman of the London Commission area or his deputy are ex-officio magistrates for all the commission areas.

High Court judges, as one might expect, continue as ex-officio justices and so do some two dozen aldermen of the City of London. The decision to retain the aldermen was reached after some serious discussion, but the outcome was that the lord mayor remains chief magistrate for the City of London, and his aldermen also retain their office. The lord mayor re-

* Abolished by the Justices of the Peace Act 1968.

mains the ex-officio chairman of the City bench and presides over that court.

QUARTER SESSIONS

Courts of quarter sessions determine the bulk of indictable offences in England—something over seventy-five per cent of the total—and they can be traced back to medieval times. Today they rank between the magistrates' courts on the lower side and the assize courts above. Their beginnings are closely associated with the justices of the peace, dealt with earlier in this chapter.

In 1327, Edward III appointed, in every county, men to keep the peace and they became known as justices. They were successors of the hundredmen; in 1388 the number of justices per county was only six. In that year, their powers and duties were formulated and they had to sit four times a year; logically their courts became known as quarter sessions which later separated from the petty sessions. The quarter sessions became a distinct court.

Those early magistrates examined persons who broke the law, and by 1360 they could hear and determine all types of criminal offence. In 1414 the dates of their sessions were fixed as the first week after Michaelmas; the first week after the Epiphany; the first week after the close of Easter; and the first week after the feast of the Translation of St Thomas the Martyr.

By the Law Terms Act of 1830 these were altered to the first week in October; the first week after 28 December; the first week after 31 March; and the first week after 24 June.

In 1925 the times of sitting were again changed and quarter sessions had to be held every year within the period of twenty-one days immediately preceding or immediately following: the twenty-fifth day of March; the twenty-fourth day of June; the twenty-ninth day of September; the twenty-fifth day of December.

Today quarter sessions must be held at least four times a year, but can be at times thought fit by the justices of a

county, or by the recorder of a borough. In addition, the
Lord Chancellor may direct more sittings, ie a court may sit
for as many days as necessary to dispose of its business. There
are two types of quarter sessions—county and borough—and
they differ slightly.

County quarter sessions

The county quarter sessions are the older of the two, and
are attended by justices from their respective county, in numbers not more than nine and not less than two. The bench is
always chaired by a legally qualified chairman. If there is more
than one court, a legally qualified deputy can act as chairman.
All justices in the county can attend but the normal sitting
is five at a time. The chairman is appointed by the queen upon
recommendations from the Lord Chancellor and is invariably
a barrister or a solicitor of at least ten years' standing. High
court judges or county court judges are chairmen in some
counties and the chairman does not have a casting vote.

In London the quarter sessions are held before a legally
qualified chairman and the minimum of two magistrates in
session does not apply. The county of London has four full-
time legally qualified chairmen who act alone in trials by jury
and preside over appeals. These chairmen retire at seventy-
two years of age.

A court of quarter sessions, sitting with a jury, has a wide
criminal jurisdiction. In addition it hears appeals of a civil
and criminal nature from decisions given in a magistrates'
court and on top of this it does have a somewhat restricted
administrative function.

In a smaller county, quarter sessions will be held at the
county town, but the justices are always drawn from magistrates' courts within their particular county. The clerk of the
peace ensures that the various provisions are complied with.
Sittings in a county may occur at different places however
and there may also be borough quarter sessions within a county
area, but held within the boundaries of the borough in question.
Scarborough, for example, in the North Riding of Yorkshire
lies within that county so Scarborough Borough Quarter

Sessions may sit at the same time as the North Riding Quarter Sessions who sit at the county town of Northallerton.

Borough quarter sessions

Borough quarter sessions are not very different from those of a county but they deal with cases committed within the borough. They may, in emergencies, deal with overflow cases from the counties and may be held more than once a quarter due to pressure of work. One main difference between these and county quarter sessions is that borough sessions are held before a recorder, and not a chairman. He is technically a magistrate and sits alone, although there may be a jury. He also hears appeals. He is usually a barrister with his own practice and is nominated by the borough but, since 1835, is appointed by the Crown on the advice of the Home Secretary. He retires at 72 but may, before reaching this age, become recorder of another borough or even be appointed as a judge of a county court. He might even become a High Court judge or stand for Parliament. (The recorderships of London, Liverpool and Manchester disqualify members from standing for Parliament). To qualify as a recorder, he must have at least five years' standing as a barrister, as opposed to the seven years required for a stipendiary magistrate.

A lay magistrate will adjudicate officially at borough quarter sessions only when it hears an appeal from a juvenile, because two magistrates from the juvenile panel sit with him. In a large city there may be assistant recorders. This enables two courts to sit simultaneously and the Crown Courts of Liverpool and Manchester, which act as both assizes and quarter sessions, have recorders who act as their judges. The recorder of a borough quarter sessions may, if the proceedings are likely to last more than three days, appoint a deputy to take a second court.

Many recorders are part-timers who combine this with their normal legal profession. The mayor may open and adjourn borough quarter sessions but takes no further part in the proceedings. If, five days before the court is due to sit, it seems likely that there will be no business, it can be cancelled.

The clerk of quarter sessions is known as the clerk of the peace and in practice is the clerk of the county or borough council.

There is right of appeal from quarter sessions to the Court of Appeal and to the House of Lords. When quarter sessions sit as an appeal court, however, the procedure varies. It hears appeals from magistrates' courts and this is done by a specially constituted appeals committee sitting without a jury. It is presided over by the chairman. Appeal lies from this committee by way of case stated, to a Divisional Court of Queen's Bench.

Because the procedure at quarter sessions is similar to that of the assizes, both are dealt with together in chapter two. Like the assizes, the abolition of quarter sessions is recommended by the *Royal Commission on Assizes and Quarter Sessions, 1966-69*.

MAGISTRATES' COURTS

History

Magistrates' courts (not quarter sessions) deal with a host of minor subjects. These include petty criminal offences, matrimonial cases, affiliation orders, adoption, the guardianship of infants, and licensing duties. They have a small jurisdiction over civil disputes. They also take the preliminary hearings of the more serious criminal offences to determine whether or not there is a case to answer at a higher court. This aspect is dealt with under the heading Examining Magistrates (see page 66). They also deal with juvenile offenders (see page 68).

The magistrates' court is a comparatively modern institution and yet, like most legal institutions, its origin is deeply rooted. Its development coincided roughly with that of quarter sessions. Both are staffed by magistrates but they are quite separate in their functions. The magistrates' court, widely but erroneously known as the police court, is perhaps the busiest court in the country, dealing with some million and a half offences every year.

Its origin lies in the primitive police systems of medieval

times when English communities were divided into 'hundreds'. The hundred first appeared when Edgar was King of Wessex and its area can be likened to the petty sessional divisions of today. Other names for this unit were wapentake, used in the north, and ward used elsewhere. It was from these hundreds that the hutesium system developed. This was better known as the hue and cry, for the law required a robbed person to chase and capture his assailant.

The Assize at Arms 1181 further enacted that all freemen between fifteen and sixty had to bear arms to preserve the peace. Fourteen years later, knights of the shire and other landed gentry were appointed as conservators of the peace. They had to ensure that the provisions of the Assize at Arms were carried out and from these men the modern magistrate and his court has evolved. Apart from their supervisory duties they were given administrative powers and the system was so successful that these influential people were given further powers and duties under the Justice of the Peace Act 1361 which is still in force. It is under this old Act that modern magistrates have the power to bind over persons to be of good behaviour; no better system has yet been devised.

Gradually the work of these early magistrates mushroomed into two distinct branches. The first was the supervision of the petty constables of the towns and of the parish constables; the second was the administration of their counties by holding quarterly meetings. The latter as we have seen, grew into quarter sessions, while the former became petty sessions. This evolution took many years, but the general format of petty sessions has changed little. The justices sat frequently and dealt with all kinds of small offences, leaving the bigger business to quarter sessions or assize courts.

In 1848 the duties of the magistrates were put into statute form and these have been altered by successive new laws. The latest major piece of legislation is the Criminal Justice Act 1967.

Some earlier Acts allowed justices, when sitting in petty sessions, to try certain indictable offences and this provision still exists. The summary trial of indictable offences was first established for adults in 1855, for stealing objects worth not more than 5s (25p). Today the more serious indictable offences which are triable at a magistrates' court must be heard by at least two justices, but a few minor cases can be decided by one. An odd number, eg three, is favoured in practice, to avoid disputes. A stipendiary magistrate, however, can decide most cases alone; in this respect his powers are far greater than those of a lay magistrate.

The need for at least two magistrates to decide serious cases stems from the nineteenth century. If the offence was a petty one, the offender would be dealt with summarily (ie at a petty sessions) which was often at a private house instead of a court. If the magistrate felt that the case was serious, he would send the accused for trial, either to quarter sessions or to the assizes.

It was not until the middle of the nineteenth century that petty sessional courts were obliged to sit in a court house. Before that in Bow Street, London, courts were held in the police station where a permanent paid justice sat. The erroneous term 'police court' stems from those days. The justice there dealt with offences which occurred in the city centre and, towards the end of the eighteeenth century, the Middlesex Justices Act appointed seven similar paid magistrates and constables. But this type of 'police court' ended in 1948.

Magistrates' courts were not within the scope of the *Report of the Royal Commission on Assizes and Quarter Sessions 1966–69*, consequently no recommendations on this subject can be included here.

Jurisdiction of magistrates' courts

A magistrates' court is defined as any justice or justices of the peace who are acting under any enactment, or by virtue of their commission, or under common law. This means that one justice acting under the above provisions, is legally a court. When acting alone, however, his powers are restricted. He can issue a summons or a warrant, he can visit any prison within his county or borough and he can order the destruction of food which he considers unfit for human consumption. In addition he can adjourn a trial, remand a prisoner in custody or on bail, and can release prisoners on bail. He may also hear offences under statutes such as the Vagrancy Act 1824, the Game Act 1831, the Town Police Clauses Act 1847, the Malicious Damage Act 1861 and several others. He cannot impose more than fourteen days imprisonment or order a person to pay more than 20s (£1). He can commit to custody a soldier or an airman who is allegedly an absentee and he can act as an examining magistrate at committal proceedings.

When sitting in numbers, there must be one magistrate to act as chairman of the bench. The word 'bench' means a sitting of magistrates or other judicial body. The chairman is elected in October by his colleagues and remains in office for one year. A number of deputy chairmen are elected at the same time and their office also lasts one year. The chairman or one of his deputies must preside at any sitting of the court (or at any meeting of the magistrates).

Unless sitting in a petty sessional court house, or in an occasional court house, the magistrates can never:

(i) Try summarily any information for an indictable offence
(ii) Hear a complaint
(iii) Try any information for an offence which is not indictable
(iv) Impose a sentence of imprisonment
(v) Hold an enquiry into the means of an offender.

An occasional court house is some place other than a petty sessional court house and which has been appointed as such by the magistrates of a county. Oddly enough, borough magistrates cannot appoint places as occasional court houses. Even so, when a court sits in one it has restricted powers, eg the maximum punishment which can be imposed is fourteen days imprisonment or an order to pay 20s (£1) which might be by way of a fine, costs or compensation. If premises are to be used as an occasional court house, public notice must be given and licensed premises can never be used.

Unless the law specifically forbids it, the magistrates must sit in open court, but there are no restrictions on the times at which they should sit. As a matter of practice, they themselves decide the days and times of their court and these are published well in advance for the information of all concerned.

Once the proceedings has started, a justice must remain for the duration and if, for any reason, he absents himself during a hearing he must take no further part. The hearing can continue if there are at least two remaining magistrates. However, a justice can leave when a trial has been adjourned, after the accused has been convicted. If the justices cannot continue a hearing once it has started, all the witnesses must be re-sworn and all must give their evidence again.

So far as the actual offences triable at these courts are concerned, they fall into five categories. The mode of procedure depends upon the classification of the offence currently before the court. The categories are as follows:

    (i) Offences purely of a summary nature
   (ii) Offences triable either on indictment or summarily
  (iii) Offences triable solely on indictment
  (iv) Indictable offences triable summarily
   (v) Summary offences triable on indictment.

Those in category (i), *offences purely of a summary nature*, form the bulk of the courts' work. They are created by statutes which lay down the mode of trial without an alternative. These are all minor offences—parking without lights, street nuisances, using motor vehicles with defective parts, liquor licensing offences and many more. The complete list is too large to include here.

Offences in category (ii), *triable either on indictment or summarily*, are known as hybrid offences because they carry two distinct and separate penalties. The creating statute will state as a punishment a choice of two independent penalties, and these depend upon the venue of the trial. It might give, for example, a maximum fine of £100 or four months imprisonment, or both, if the offence is tried summarily (ie before a magistrates' court). The alternative might be two years imprisonment if the offence is tried on indictment (ie before a jury at either assizes or quarter sessions).

If someone over fourteen years of age is charged with such an offence the court will proceed as if the offence is *not* a summary one, but the prosecution may ask to have it dealt with summarily. Even when they start a case as being indictable, in which event the magistrates act as examining magistrates (see page 66), they can, of their own motion, decide to try it summarily and would thereupon cease to act as examining magistrates. On these occasions, they may hear representations from the accused and the prosecution, and must consider the nature of the charge. Similarly, having started proceedings as a summary trial, the justices can, before the end of the prosecution evidence, discontinue the hearing and then act as examining magistrates.

For any hybrid offence which carries more than three months imprisonment on summary conviction, an accused can request trial by jury. Many of them do this. Invariably trial by jury means risking a higher punishment, yet some consider it a fairer method. The decision rests with the accused —it is a gamble he takes.

Offences in category (iii) *triable solely on indictment*, consists of common law offences and some created by statute which do not permit summary trial. These are heard either at assizes or quarter sessions; some can be heard at the assizes only. Murder is a good example because it cannot be dealt with by the magistrates, although a murder trial, like any other, always begins in a magistrates' court before the examining magistrates. They decide whether or not there is sufficient evidence to send the accused for trial; they do not decide innocence or guilt.

Category (iv) offences, *indictable offences triable summarily*, are listed in Schedule 1 of the Magistrates Courts Act 1952. If an offence is not listed there, it cannot be dealt with in this manner, but the list is too extensive to incorporate here. Examples include: theft, malicious damage, indecent assault, some forgeries, some perjuries, indecent publications, etc.

If a person is charged with such an offence, which could be tried at either assizes or quarter sessions, he can be dealt with at a magistrates' court, *but only if he consents*. The court, however, must tell him that he has the right to be tried by a jury, and furthermore they must inform him that although he has consented to a summary trial he might, upon conviction, be sent to a higher court (ie quarter sessions) to be sentenced.

To determine the method of trial of such an offence, various considerations must be made. If, during an enquiry into such an offence allegedly committed by a person seventeen years of age or over, representations are made by either the prosecution or the defence for it to be tried summarily, the court will take heed of the suitable punishment, the seriousness of the charge and whether there are other reasons to make trial on indictment unsuitable. If these points are satisfied, the trial can proceed before the magistrates. Alternatively, if summary proceedings have already started, the justices may, before hearing all the prosecution evidence, decide to treat the case as indictable in which case they would at that stage act as examining magistrates.

A person convicted by the magistrates of such an offence cannot be sentenced to more than six months imprisonment, or to a fine exceeding £100 or both. The disposal of these cases is entirely at the discretion of the magistrates, with the exception of cases affecting the property or affairs of the sovereign, or of a public body. In these cases, the prosecutor must consent and this also applies where the Director of Public Prosecutions is the prosecutor.

Occasionally a person is convicted by the magistrates of such an offence, but they feel that the punishment which they can award is inadequate. The magistrates therefore commit the convicted person to quarter sessions to be sentenced there, because quarter sessions can impose higher sentences. This only applies to offences carrying three months or more imprisonment because they give right of trial by jury.

Offences in category (v), *summary offences triable on indict-*

ment, consists of those for which summary trial is provided but which in certain cases may be dealt with on indictment. Generally speaking, these are offences for which a person over the age of fourteen can receive a sentence of three months imprisonment and for which he may therefore claim trial by jury. It does not include assault, or offences of living on the immoral earnings of prostitution, controlling a prostitute and soliciting by men for immoral purposes. In these cases, the prosecution can *send* an accused for trial; he cannot ask for this.

Procedure at magistrates' courts

An accused person may appear before the magistrates either through being arrested and charged, or through receipt of a summons. An arrested person will usually stand in the dock, whilst a person who has been summoned to attend for a minor offence will perhaps stand at the bar of the court or, in the absence of a bar, on the floor in front of the magisterial bench.

The magistrates' clerk will read the precise charge and, if the trial is a summary one, will ask for a plea. This should be either guilty or not guilty, but occasions do arise when a person adds something in mitigation which suggests that a not guilty plea is correct. It even happens that the defendant himself is not aware of this—he pleads guilty and begins to give reasons which could amount to not guilty. Any doubtful plea *must* be treated as not guilty and the full facts will be heard and decided by the court.

If the *prosecution* have the right to elect for summary trial, the election must be made after the charge has been put to the defendant, but before anything else. It must certainly come before the plea. If, on the other hand, the *defendant* has the right to claim trial by jury, the magistrates' clerk will inform him of his rights after the charge has been read. Other information, such as the possibility of a committal to quarter sessions for sentence, must also be given to the defendant and he will have to decide his type of hearing.

Upon electing for a summary trial his plea will be taken

and the proceedings will begin. If he goes for trial by jury, there will be no plea, because the justices thereupon become examining magistrates and committal proceedings will begin. The accused thus begins his journey either to quarter sessions or the assizes for trial.

When a person pleads guilty at the magistrates' court, the prosecution will outline the case and inform the court of any points of law involved. The police witnesses may then give details of any previous convictions and the accused person can question witnesses if facts are in dispute. An advocate may speak on his behalf and ask the questions. Afterwards, either the defendant or his advocate can address the court in an effort to mitigate the penalty.

The bench then decides the appropriate penalty. If it is a fine, he can be given time to pay. If it is a short sentence of imprisonment, they can grant bail if the defence gives notice of appeal. A magistrates' court can, since 1 January 1968, give a suspended sentence, ie a short term of imprisonment which is suspended for an operational period. The operational period can vary between one and three years, but during that time the defendant must behave himself. If he does not, he may be sent back to court and may actually have to serve the original suspended sentence in addition to any further punishment for his latest offence.

Where the term of imprisonment is not more than six months in respect of one offence, the sentence *must* be suspended unless:

(i) The offences consisted of an assault or threat of violence to another person, or of having or possessing a firearm, imitation firearm, explosive or offensive weapon, or of indecent conduct with or towards a person under sixteen

(ii) The offence is one where a probation order, or an order for a conditional discharge was originally made, or the offender was subject to such an order at the time of committing such offence

(iii) The court wishes to pass or proposes to pass an im-

mediate sentence of imprisonment for another offence
which the court is not required to suspend

(iv) The offender is serving or has served a sentence of
imprisonment or borstal training previously passed
for another offence

(v) The offender had at any time before the commission
of the offence been sentenced to, or served, any part
of a sentence of corrective training, imprisonment or
borstal training previously passed for another offence
or been subject to a suspended sentence.

The above does not *prevent* the courts imposing suspended
sentences in the above instances; it merely allows them discretion.

For a not guilty plea, however, the procedure is not so
simple. The prosecution must establish beyond all reasonable
doubt that the defendant is guilty. After the plea, the case
is opened by the prosecution, whose speech must contain
all the necessary and relevant details. After the prosecutor
has spoken (he is often a police officer) he will call his witnesses
who wait outside the court. This is to prevent them
hearing other evidence and being influenced by it. Each will
take the oath and will give an account of events or produce
exhibits or documentary evidence to establish a case against
the defendant. When all have given their evidence the accused
may, through his advocate if desired, submit that there is no
case to answer. The prosecution can reply to this. If the court
upholds such a submission, the case will end; the defendant
will be discharged and allowed to go home.

When the prosecution has concluded, the defence takes over.
If there are no witnesses, reliance will be placed on the speech
given at the conclusion of the defence case. Normally the defence
will produce witnesses who have waited outside and they
will give evidence on oath. The defendant, who has listened to
all the evidence for and against him, may be called to give
evidence. He is not obliged to do so, and may therefore decline.
He would normally give it after the prosecution witnesses
and before his own. After the defence witnesses comes the

E

defence speech, although it could be given before the defence witnesses are called. It is normally delivered after their evidence because it then carries more weight. With leave of the court, both the prosecution and the defence may make two speeches.

After this the magistrates decide the case and may retire to a private room to discuss it. They are not assisted but can seek advice on points of law from the magistrates' clerk. He must never help them to make a decision.

If they deliver a not guilty verdict, the defendant will be discharged and may go home, although he can seek costs before leaving the court. This is entirely in the hands of the court, who may refuse costs.

If the finding is one of guilty then, before announcing sentence, the bench will ask for details of the accused's previous character which may affect his sentence. If he has convictions, these must on no account be made known to the magistrates before their verdict, unless the accused himself introduces them, or unless they are permitted by statute to be given, as for example, in a trial on a charge of handling stolen goods. When these personal details are known, the magistrates will award their punishment.

For details of appeals against a magistrates' court decision, see chapter six.

EXAMINING MAGISTRATES

The term examining magistrates is given to the justices of a petty sessional court who conduct proceedings which are preliminary to a trial by jury. These are known as committal proceedings and during them the magistrates do not determine the accused's guilt or innocence; instead they listen to the evidence and decide in their own minds whether there is a case to answer. If they find insufficient evidence to commit a person for trial, he will be discharged. If, on the other hand, the examining magistrates feel that there is a case, they will commit the accused for trial at the next quarter sessions or assizes. He can be committed either in custody or on bail.

Examining magistrates must sit in open court unless statutorily prohibited, or unless they feel that the interests of justice will be defeated. Committal proceedings can take place almost anywhere, even in a hospital or a prison, but in practice they are heard in a court house. The functions of examining magistrates can be carried out by one magistrate sitting alone.

Every indictable offence must be investigated by examining magistrates to determine whether there is a *prima facie* case to be sent for trial. This does not apply however when the accused is committed without consideration of the evidence as is now permitted by the Criminal Justice Act 1967, and it does not necessarily apply when the offence is:

(i) One which may be and is dealt with summarily

(ii) One for which an offender is committed for trial on a coroner's inquisition

(iii) On an indictment preferred by order of a judge of the High Court, or under section 9 of the Perjury Act 1911.

Committal proceedings are sometimes criticised because of the time involved, but for a defendant there are two good reasons to support them. The first is that a defendant may not have a long wait for a trial—lack of evidence against him will result in a dismissal by the examining magistrates. Secondly, it does enable a defendant to get a copy of the prosecution evidence and so have time to consider it before a trial.

Prior to the Criminal Justice Act 1967 committal proceedings were a ponderous process because the evidence was taken down on a typewriter or by long-hand during the actual proceedings. Such statements were always on oath before the court and had to be signed by the person making them and by the justice. These were and still are known as depositions, ie 'a statement made on oath before a justice, taken down in writing in the presence and hearing of the accused and read over to the deponent or the person making it, and by the justice'. It is a record of the evidence given by each witness and remains in the care of the magistrate's clerk until required at the subsequent trial before a jury.

One effect of the Criminal Justice Act 1967 was to abolish, to a certain extent, time-wasting depositions. Instead, a person can now be committed for trial without consideration of the evidence. Secondly, written statements, not made on oath, can be used in lieu of oral evidence if certain conditions are observed. By use of these new procedures, time is saved and the functions of the examining magistrates have been reduced; the administration of justice is speeded up.

DOMESTIC COURTS

For domestic proceedings, a magistrates' court must consist of not more than three justices who should be representative of both sexes. The proceedings should be separated from the other business and the public are not admitted.

The types of case dealt with are usually applications for maintenance of wives and/or children whether legitimate or not; separation orders, affiliation orders, custody of children, applications to marry by infants and certain proceedings relating to family allowances.

The magistrates' involvement with this type of civil judicial work dates from the Poor Law of Elizabeth I. In those times, justices administered parish relief and this work, which resembles that old relief, has evolved into its present form.

JUVENILE COURTS

One of the first statutes to deal specifically with children came into force in 1847 and allowed lay justices to try at their own courts thieves under the age of fourteen. Hitherto the justices had to commit such offenders to a High Court for trial before a judge and jury. Some thirty years later, the Summary Jurisdiction Act 1879 made it possible for the majority of cases involving children to be deal with by the justices.

Following this legislation, many magistrates dealt separately with juveniles even though they were not legally bound to do so. But the real beginning of the juvenile court came with an Act of Parliament known as the 'Children's Charter'. This was the Children Act 1908. It established the children's court, later known as the juvenile court. Today there are about 820 juvenile courts in England and Wales, with some 8,500 justices on their panels.

The establishment of these courts was only the beginning. Convicted children could still be sent to prison where they came into contact with mature criminals. This state of affairs persisted as late as 1922 in some remand prisons. After that time, all those under twenty-one were segregated from adult offenders.

Formerly, though, the courts which dealt with young offenders consisted of ordinary magistrates with no special knowledge or interest in juveniles. The practice of selecting particular justices began in London in 1920. These courts were served by a stipendiary magistrate nominated by the Home Office, and he sat with two lay justices, one of whom had to be a woman. In 1936, the position changed to allow selected lay magistrates to take the chair in the London juvenile courts. The selected lay magistrates system applied, and still applies, to the rest of England.

The next step came in 1928 with the report of the Prison Commissioners. This criticised the courts' practice of sending to prison young persons who could be dealt with under the Probation Act or else sent to Borstal. During 1928, for example, 1,721 boys and 128 girls received prison sentences. Even as late as the 1930s, children were still being sent to prison or remanded in prison to await a sentence which was often probation.

The most important year for children in trouble was 1933. In that year the Children and Young Persons Act 1933 came into operation and laid down, in no uncertain way, the ideals to be aimed at by the juvenile courts which had then been operating for a quarter of a century. The Act says that when a child or young person is brought before a court either as being in need of care or protection, or as an offender, or for any other reason, the court must consider the welfare of the child or young person. It shall take steps to remove him from undesirable surroundings and to ensure that proper provision is made for his education and training.

With this Act, therefore, the emphasis shifted from punishment to reform and another important aspect was to fix, in statute form, the age of criminal responsibility. The Act said that no child under the age of 8 could be guilty of any offence.

Common law had put the age at 7: here it was raised to 8 and today the age is 10. This latest increase occurred on 1 February 1964 under the provisions of the Children and Young Persons Act 1963. There is every possibility that the age will be increased still further, possibly to 14 in the 1970s. As long ago as 1883, it was suggested that the age of criminal responsibility be 12 except for atrocious crimes. One current suggestion is that it corresponds with school-leaving age. In some European countries the age is 16 or even 18, whilst in one part of the USA it is 21.

The age groups which can be dealt with by an English juvenile court are strictly laid down: they are divided into *children* and *young persons*. Children are those under 14 and young persons are between 14 and 17. They are collectively known as *juveniles* in judicial circles, but the word has no legal backing—it is simply a word of convenience.

The juvenile courts cannot deal with anyone over seventeen; such offenders must be dealt with at the adult magistrates' court. There are a few exceptions to this rule. If a person appearing before a juvenile court is suddenly found to be over seventeen, the court may continue to hear and determine the case. Again, if a juvenile has been made the subject of a probation order or perhaps a conditional discharge, he can be dealt with in respect of any breach of such orders by the juvenile court which made them, after he attains the age of seventeen.

Without doubt, the age group which causes most judicial concern is that known as children, ie those under fourteeen. The law recognises that there is a stage when children are morally responsible as individuals, whilst the same does not apply to children as a group. Only if a child *knows* his act to be wrong, can he be guilty, and only then should he be punished. It is most difficult for a juvenile court to decide the correct course of action with children of this age, for it must be proved that they *knew* they were doing wrong. This knowledge of wrong is most difficult to prove.

Some juvenile courts openly accept that all children under fourteen do not know when they have committed an offence and acquit them all. Claude Mullins in his *Crime and Psychology* records one such court which acquitted almost every child who came before it. The snag was that a problem child might be deprived of expert help and so his mistakes might never be corrected. In contrast to this court, it is of interest to consider some examples of the progressive twentieth century!

In 1938 a boy of 13 was tried for murder but was acquitted at the Central Criminal Court after an argument about his *knowledge of wrong*. He was later sent to an approved school by a juvenile court. In 1947 an assize court judge sentenced a 9 year-old boy to five years detention for manslaughter and the little chap was dealt with in only eight minutes. He had pleaded guilty to the crime and this case established that such a plea from a child could be accepted without any further evidence (*R. v Thomas 1947. 111 J.P.Jo.669*). In 1958, only a decade or so ago, an 8 year-old boy was charged with housebreaking. In 1959 a boy of 12 admitted he knew what was meant by stealing. This was accepted as evidence of his *knowledge of wrong*. In the same year, a boy of 8 was convicted of house-breaking when he broke into a house and stole cash. His guilty knowledge was proved because he threw the cashbox into a water tank and admitted stealing it.

Constitution and jurisdiction

As well as establishing the ages of youngsters to be dealt with at juvenile courts, the 1933 Act went on to formulate the constitution of those courts, and to lay down their powers.

The panel of magistrates for a juvenile court is chosen from those who normally sit in the adult court, but usually such magistrates have a special interest in juveniles or are skilled at dealing with them. They cannot serve on the juvenile panel after reaching the age of 65 (with the exception of a stipendiary magistrate). They may only serve for three years at a time. There are slight variations between London and the provinces. In London the panel of magistrates and the chairman are nominated by the Home Secretary for the juvenile courts in the Metropolis. Outside the City of London and the Metropolitan Police Court area, the juvenile panel must consist of not more than three magistrates and, since 1954, must include at least one man and one woman. Power is given for a stipendiary magistrate to sit alone on a juvenile bench in certain circumstances and, of course, any juvenile court magistrate may sit in an adult court, as indeed they often do.

A juvenile court must always be held in a room or building quite separate from the ordinary courts, and it must sit at different times. In the larger court houses there is often a spare court room which can be used as a juvenile court, although often an ante-room or even a large office is utilised. If an ordinary court room is used, at least one hour must elapse between the adult court and the juvenile court. This is to prevent juveniles from becoming acquainted with adult courts and this even extends to the language used. Words like conviction and sentence must not be used in a juvenile court and the charge must always be explained in simple language. When taking the oath, a child must promise to tell the truth—he must never swear, because so many youngsters place the wrong interpretation on that word.

Further to protect juvenile defendants, these courts are not open to the general public, although the press is allowed to take note of the proceedings on condition that the defendant's name, address, school or other particulars calculated to lead to his identification are omitted from their reports. In special circumstances, however, the court or the Secretary of State may allow publication of these particulars if it is in the interests of justice.

Only certain persons are allowed in a juvenile court. These include the accused youngster and his parents or guardian, the police (who may wear civilian clothes), the probation officer who will have been informed via the police channels, and a representative of the children's department of the local authority. In addition there will be the magistrates, their clerk and perhaps a solicitor acting for the accused juvenile. Witnesses may be present and so must persons concerned in the proceedings; the court may authorise others to be present at its discretion.

Just as these restrictions are placed on a juvenile court, so are its powers limited. It can never sentence anyone to imprisonment and every child under fourteen must be dealt with at a juvenile court, no matter what his offence. The only exception is homicide; for this even a child under fourteen must go for trial at the assizes.

The fines imposed by a juvenile court are limited; a child under fourteen may be fined up to £10, a young person between fourteen and seventeen can be fined up to £50. On top of this, costs or damages up to £100 may be imposed.

The court may find a juvenile not guilty and will then discharge him. The penalties it may impose on conviction include an absolute discharge (which is a conviction), a conditional discharge for not more than three years, probation, committal to the care of a fit person, a term in a detention centre, or visits to an attendance centre. A person over sixteen may be sent to prison, but not by a juvenile court; this would be done at the assizes, for example.

Occasionally, a child under ten does appear before a juvenile court, but this would not be in respect of any criminal offence. It would arise when the child was thought to be in need of care, protection or control, and the court would make an order according to its findings.

A child or young person thought to be in need of care, protection or control can be brought before a juvenile court by the local authority, the police, or some other authorised person such as an officer of the NSPCC. If an order is made, the child can be committed to the care of a fit person, sent to an approved school or to a hospital.

If a parent thinks his child is beyond control, he must ask the local authority to take proceedings on his behalf. This safeguard is necessary because some parents had their own children put into homes through this method. If, however, the local authority does nothing upon such a request, the parents can make a direct approach to the court and their plea will be heard.

Procedure

The procedure at a juvenile court is the same as that in the adult court, already described, except that there is far less formality. However, the provisions of the Children and Young Person's Act 1969 may result in changes in juvenile courts. Care, protection or control proceedings will be replaced by care proceedings; approved school orders and fit person orders will be replaced by care orders, and there will be new provisions governing the supervision of children and young persons on probation. These are expected to become effective on 1 October 1970, although no date has (at the time of writing) been fixed for changes in the power to prosecute children and young persons.

FOUR
Civil Courts

THE COUNTY COURTS

There are about 400 county courts in England and Wales and in very broad terms they can be likened to the magistrates' courts in that the latter is the lowest criminal court and the county court is the lowest civil court. It must not be forgotten, however, that magistrates may occasionally deal with limited civil matters. In addition to this modern comparison, the medieval county courts (from which the present ones are *not* descended) had barristers as their judges. This was rather like the modern recorder of a borough. In some, though, the judges were aldermen and mayors, which again is similar to our justices and the now disappearing ex-officio justices.

During the Anglo-Saxon period, courts known as schyremotes were held in the English shires twice a year. On the bench were the bishop and the eldermen (ealdermen) or the sheriff and, in Canute's time (1017-35), the schyremotes were held three times a year. Edward the Confessor in 1065 appointed them to be held twelve times a year. When presided over by the sheriff, these old courts could deal with criminal matters; the modern county court, on the other hand, has no criminal jurisdiction at all.

Towards the end of the Middle Ages those old county courts had very little work because many boroughs and cities possessed valid charters which gave them power to hold local courts. These had a variety of names such as mayor's court, sheriff's court, bailiff's court and many others. Although the power of these ancient courts were very fluid, their jurisdiction was generally limited to areas within the boundaries of the parent borough.

When, with the growth of industry, new towns expanded and multiplied, it was discovered that these areas did not possess old charters which meant they had no local courts. Jurisdiction of the courts in the county areas did not apply and so, in the eighteenth and nineteenth centuries, an effort was made through private Bills in Parliament, to establish small courts in these new towns to cope with minor civil pleas. Such courts were eventually established. Their jurisdiction was limited to actions for debt where the amount at issue did not exceed 40s (£2) and the court consisted of a bench of men whose status was equivalent to that of the local justices. These courts were to be accessible to anyone with a civil problem irrespective of their financial status; indeed many of them operated under the revived title of Court of Requests (see page 178). Some were called courts of conscience.

But as these new courts became established within the growing boroughs, it was realised that the counties had no such courts, ie courts to which anyone could plead irrespective of their status in the community, or their financial position. They still had their old local courts with their limited jurisdiction. An attempt to rectify this was made in 1750 by reorganising the Middlesex County Courts, and the efforts proved successful. The courts were held by the county clerk with a jury of twelve freeholders, and the amount in issue did not exceed 40s (£2). From this beginning grew the present system of county courts. But it was not until 1846, almost a century later, that the County Courts Act became law. This was the most important statute governing these brand new courts and, under its provisions, each county was split into several county court districts. There were fifty-nine circuits in England and Wales and they remain to this day.

The name county court was chosen because the court embraced persons living in a county area, but it is misleading. The jurisdiction of these courts is not necessarily limited to county boundaries and the judge of a county court now works on a circuit basis when operating outside a large city. He visits

each court within his circuit about once a month and his visits
are very similar to those of the sheriffs who toured the hundreds so long ago.

The judge of a county court, who is addressed as 'your
Honour', has to be a barrister of at least seven years standing
and is appointed by the Lord Chancellor. The judges in the
Duchy of Lancaster are appointed by the chancellor of the
duchy, and any county court judge can be removed for dis-
ability or misbehaviour. They normally retire at 72, but this
can be extended to 75.

In 1934 there were 60 judges; in 1955 the number was increased to 80 and the figure of 90 was achieved in 1964. In
1969, it was increased to 105. They are all justices of the
peace and can act as chairmen of quarter sessions; they all
try divorce cases and many sit on royal commissions. In the
early days, a county court judge always sat with a jury, but
juries are rarely seen in modern county courts.

When these courts were established by the County Courts
Act 1846, they were to be used for 'an easy recovery of small
debts and demands in England'. The jurisdiction of the early
county courts was limited to £20 which was an increase over
the amounts which had existed since 1278, ie 40s (£2). The
Act was amended in 1849, following which their jurisdiction
was extended in 1850 to suits for sums not exceeding £50.
Further amendments occurred during the next nine years and,
by an Act passed in 1859, the county court could only commit for trial where credit had been obtained by fraud or breach
of trust. England and Wales was, at that time, divided into
sixty districts, exclusive of London, and these could be en-
larged or reduced by the sovereign in council. Courts were
held in the majority of towns at least once every calendar
month. In 1865, the County Courts Equitable Jurisdiction Act
gave them powers of a court of chancery in suits by creditors,
legatees, divorcees, heirs at law or next of kin, and also in
cases of legal procedure concerning estates not exceeding £500
in value.

The county courts of today, however, bear little resemblance
to those founded in 1846 by Lord Brougham. He had a diffi-

cult task to see his idea reach fruition due to opposition from
the legal profession, but won in the end. He created these
courts to cope with small cases, and as places where poor
litigants could win justice. Prior to this, they had to take their
action to Westminster, or await the assizes. As the crown
courts expanded to deal with nearly all civil matters, these
ancient local courts fell into disuse which meant there was
little or no provision for small pleas by the poor. The Court of
Requests had ceased in 1642. Some local courts did survive
and still exist today, ie the Bristol Tolzey Court, the Norwich
Guildhall Court, the Salford Hundred Court and the Liverpool
Court of Passage, all of which deal with a moderate amount
of business.

Apart from the judge, each court has a registrar. He is really
in charge of the office and is a solicitor, although he can act
as judge at his own court in smaller disputes. He may act for
more than one court and is appointed and removable by the
Lord Chancellor.

County courts deal with the following matters:

(i) Actions founded on contract and tort (except libel,
slander, seduction and breach of promise of marriage),
but there are financial limitations. Prior to 1939, the
limit was £100. In 1938 it was raised to £200 subject
to a proviso that a defendant who sued for not more
than £100 could object to the jurisdiction and so
compel the plaintiff to go to the High Court. In 1955
the limit was increased again to £400, with a proviso
that it could be made £500 by an Order in Council.
This order was made. Since 1966 the limit has been
£500, and at the time of writing, legislation is before
Parliament to raise it to £750. The *Report of the Royal
Commission on Assizes and Quarter Sessions 1966-69*
recommends that this amount be £1,000. (The parties
to an action can consent to the county court having
jurisdiction even where the amount involved is larger
than the county court limit)

(ii) Equity matters such as trusts, mortgages, dissolution

of partnerships where the amount does not exceed £500

(iii) Actions concerning land (including houses and other buildings) where the net value for rating does not exceed £400

(iv) Limited Admiralty jurisdiction in some courts. The claim must not exceed £1,000 except a claim for salvage where the value of the salvaged property must not exceed £3,500

(v) Bankruptcies (in certain courts outside the London Bankruptcy District). There is also jurisdiction in the winding up of companies with a paid-up capital not exceeding £10,000

(vi) There is jurisdiction over proceedings transferred from the High Court

(vii) Special statutory jurisdiction. This includes subjects such as guardianship of infants, housing, adoptions, landlord and tenant, legitimacy and similar subjects.

County courts do not deal with matrimonial cases, bastardy or criminal matters, although there is power to commit a person to prison for contempt of court. All divorces begin in the county court; undefended ones are usually completed here.

The London county courts are similar to those in the provinces, with the possible exception of the Mayor's and City of London court. This is held in the Guildhall and is a combination of older courts. When functioning as the City of London court, its jurisdiction is akin to that of a county court; as Mayor's court, however, it has unlimited jurisdiction in actions of tort and contract and some other matters. The *Royal Commission on Assizes and Quarter Sessions 1966–69* recommends the abolition of the unlimited jurisdiction of this court, and suggests that it serve purely as a county court for the City.

Procedure

Juries may, but seldom do, sit in a county court. The hearings are divided between registrars and judges. A registrar takes the lesser cases such as those where a defendant admits the claim. However, he can hear defended cases if there is no objection from either party and provided the claim does not exceed £30. He can take cases involving higher amounts with the consent of both parties. In practice, many cases are withdrawn before reaching the court and judgements are made without a hearing, or even in the defendant's absence.

The procedure in court is very similar to that of the higher civil courts which is to be found later in this chapter.

BANKRUPTCY COURTS

The word 'bankrupt' is derived through the French from the Latin *bancus*=the counter, and *ruptus*=broken. Persons who went bankrupt in ancient times were regarded as having committed a very severe wrong and the Roman Law of the Twelve Tables gave creditors the power to cut a debtor's body into small pieces, each receiving a proportionate share. The modern sharing of assets is perhaps more constructive!

In those times too, there were other punishments. Debtors could be imprisoned in chains, or subjected to whipping and hard labour, and were even liable to be sold abroad (with their wives and children). As long ago as 326 BC, these laws were relaxed by the *Lex Poetelia Papira*, and in Rome subsequent Christian emperors introduced a law by which a person giving up all his goods was exempted from penalties. This became known as *Cessio bonorum*.

In England, however, the first statute to deal with this was created in 1542 and became effective in 1543 during the reign of Henry VIII. It guarded against frauds by traders, particularly those who obtained goods then fled overseas without paying. The Act gave power to the Lord Chancellor and other high officials to seize estates and other assets, which they could share between creditors. The Act provided no relief to the bankrupt person but gradually the situation changed to allow a person to obtain his discharge with or without the debtor's consent, provided he conformed to the bankruptcy laws.

In Henry's time, though, fraudulent dealing was a criminal offence and a felony and as such carried the death penalty. But Elizabeth I confined bankruptcy to traders. She gave the chancellor power to appoint persons to supervise the property of a bankrupt person. Tough legislation was continued by James I who, in 1624, extended the offence of bankruptcy to include scriveners. This Act said that, unless the bankrupt's debts had occurred from some accidental cause, he could be sent to the pillory for two hours and have one of his ears cut off. In addition, he could be nailed to the pillory. This Act was not repealed until 1816!

In 1732, George II extended the bankruptcy laws to include bankers and, later, farmers, factory owners and brokers. Even aliens did not escape the laws and soon they included most business people. George's statute gave the chancellor direct control over bankruptcy matters.

In 1825 all the minor Acts were consolidated and commissioners were appointed to enforce the bankruptcy laws; even so there were many more amendments and consolidations until the Bankruptcy Act 1854. A few years before, a new bankruptcy court had been built by William IV. This had been opened in 1831, the year Lord Brougham became Lord Chancellor and was designed to relieve the Court of Chancery or the Chancery Division of its bankruptcy work. During this period, imprisonment was still a penalty which could be inflicted on debtors. However, the Debtors Act 1869 abolished this, although it gave no protection to fraudulent bankrupts. After this Act, the bankruptcy laws were enforced by two Chancery Division judges assisted by registrars. Today, bankruptcy is a purely civil matter although some criminal offences are closely connected, eg financial frauds. The movement to standardise bankruptcy procedure led eventually to a further Bankruptcy Act in 1914 which is still in force.

The objects of these laws are to distinguish between a true inability to meet obligations and a deliberate refusal or neglect to do so. The laws also try to share the debtor's assets between his creditors and prevent one gaining unfair advantage over another. Priorities like wages and tax must be remembered.

F

Procedure

An action for alleged bankruptcy can begin with an execution of judgement on the debtor's property, followed by the service of a notice of bankruptcy. If the debtor fails to satisfy the judgement within a week, proceedings may begin. The creditor proceeds by petition in a bankruptcy court, providing he is entitled to at least £50. The petition is served on the debtor who may either deny the allegation of debt or otherwise oppose it. The procedure from this point is controlled by the registrars and this pertains whether the case is for the High Court or a county court. When a receiving order is made, a debtor must list all his assets and must appear before the appropriate court for his public examination. If he does not appear, he can be arrested. The creditors place their claims before the court and these must be proved to its satisfaction.

A debtor may, if he wishes, ask his creditors to accept a 'composition' by which he can pay part of the outstanding amount and pay the rest later. By this method he could carry on his business under supervision, but the acceptance of a composition depends upon a majority agreement by all the creditors involved and, in addition, upon leave of the court. In the event of a minority disagreement, there is right of appeal to the Court of Appeal (Civil Division). If the creditors will not accept a composition, the debtor may be declared bankrupt.

A trustee in bankruptcy will then be appointed and all the bankrupt's property will be vested in him. He must collate it and can sue persons who owe money to the bankrupt. The bankrupt's assets are eventually divided between his creditors according to a strict rule of priorities. When some of his debts have been met, the bankrupt can apply to the registrar for his discharge. His application may be heard either by the registrar or by a judge, and there is right of appeal against this decision. It lies to the Court of Appeal (Civil Division). A discharge may be conditional, in that he makes further payments out of future earnings, and such discharge never absolves the bankrupt from debts which were not subject of the bankruptcy hearing.

An undischarged bankrupt is restricted in his activities: he cannot, for example, obtain credit to the extent of £10 or more without informing the person that he is an undischarged bankrupt, nor can he engage in any trade or business without informing persons with whom he enters into any transaction. There is a penalty of up to two years imprisonment for contravention of these provisions. An undischarged bankrupt must not risk further insolvency by gambling, or making rash speculations, and he must keep proper accounts. He must not abscond with his property.

CHANCERY DIVISION OF THE HIGH COURT

This court has evolved from the time when the Lord Chancellor, one of the land's highest officials, took a major share in the work of the king's council. Even when the council was not in session, he had a court of his own to which he could compel witnesses to attend and give evidence. His court was flexible: it dealt with matters beyond its legal jurisdiction which gave him and his court some very strong powers, even though their legality was doubted. This sort of thing occurred frequently in medieval times—the precise jurisdiction of any court was never very clear.

Long before the establishment of Chancery, the office of chancellor was in existence. It may have been instituted by Alfred the Great in AD 887, or even before then; one suggested date is AD 605, although many authorities accept that the years 1067–70 are the most likely. The office is said to have continued without a break since 1066, and was originally of a secretarial nature. Even in the time of the Curia Regis (see page 174), the chancellor undertook some judicial work but his real role in the legal world began with the establishment of the Court of Exchequer.

Initially, the office of chancellor was bestowed upon a religious dignitary known as *cancellarius*, or door-keeper. This name comes from the *cancelli* or screen behind which the secretarial work of the royal household took place. This person was always an ecclesiastic in charge of the royal chaplains and administered the royal monies. It was also his duty to admit visitors to the king's presence and he was, in effect, a secretary of state for all departments, with powers given to him by the king's council. It was a long time before he became head of the English judicial system. As his work and responsibilities increased, he employed clerks and divided his work into departments; he became head of the Chancery which was separated from the Exchequer in 1199.

It must be remembered that the king's word was law, but to be effective, royal pronunciations had to be circulated to the public. One of the chancellor's duties was to compile the neccessary documents and these were known as writs. They bore the royal seal, often called the great seal, which was kept by the chancellor. His staff wrote them and sealed them on a marble table close to the marble bench which stood in Westminster Hall. This marble bench was the king's bench, and as we have seen, this gave its name to the King's Bench Division of the High Court.

The chancellor really enters the legal system through some early appeals. Decisions by assizes and the common law courts were considered harsh, even in the early middle ages, and there was always right of redress through the king in person. To hear these, he sat with his council and, because large numbers of appeals came to the king, the chancellor (his door-keeper) had to sift them. He received the applicants and, being an ecclesiastic, it was felt he would be fair. He dealt personally with some minor appeals and passed the rest to the king, although all decisions were made in the king's name.

Whether the decisions were made by the king and his council, or by the chancellor, they were invariably based on moral issues rather than legal ones. It was from this that equity grew. Eventually, all pleas were addressed to the chancellor—this had occurred by the thirteenth century. If he felt there was a case to answer, he would summon an alleged offender to appear before him. Apart from this, no person having any interest in a case could give evidence on his own behalf in a court of common law. This was changed in 1843.

When the chancellor began to hear direct petitions, successive chancellors followed suit and each based his ruling upon those of his predecessors. This led to the system of rules and precedents being established and eventually, about 1340, the chancellor became a judge in his own court—the Court of Chancery. Perhaps it was named after him, or after the *cancelli*, in this case a bar of open timber-work which separated this court from the lower part of Westminster Hall, where it was housed in the south-west corner. The first register of writs goes back to 1227, but there are records of Chancery proceedings dating back to the reign of Richard II (1377-99). By the fourteenth century, this was a very powerful court.

In the court sat the Lord Chancellor with the Master of the Rolls (who sometimes acted as deputy to the Lord Chancellor) and eleven other men with knowledge of civil law. When assembled they were known as Masters in Chancery. Of these, the Master of the Rolls was, in the fifteenth century, known as the Keeper of the State Rolls and he was then a minor official who looked after court documents. They were kept in rolls or pipes, hence their name. Sometimes they were known as pipe rolls. Like so many minor posts, his importance grew until, by the seventeenth century, he was a judge who could hear equity cases. Later he became President of the Court of Appeal, ranking third in the judicial hierarchy—the Lord Chancellor and the Lord Chief Justice are above him. The Master of the Rolls was no longer a mere clerk.

Eventually, the post of Lord Chancellor ceased to be drawn from ecclesiastics; instead, persons with a legal knowledge were appointed. The last clerical chancellor was Bishop Williams who held office in the reigns of James I and Charles I. The last one not to practise law was Lord Shaftesbury in 1672.

The chancery court, which was of a purely civil nature, differed from the criminal courts in that it tried to correct all wrongs, rather than to punish for crime. As the chancellor gained more power, however, he did try to acquire business from other courts, but his attempts were challenged with the result that his jurisdiction was kept within its limits. Today those problems have disappeared and the jurisdiction of every court is defined.

The modern chancery court deals with the administration of estates including those of deceased persons, partnerships and mortgages, contractual rights, execution of trusts and settlements, and the wardship of infants. It also hears appeals and deals with the winding-up of certain companies, as well as having some jurisdiction over bankruptcy. Persons wishing to bring an action before Chancery must now make their approach through the High Court, of which Chancery is part, although in Lancashire and Durham there are local chancery courts (see page 153).

Procedure

Chancery proceedings are so varied that it is difficult to generalise. Some cases are heard in chambers and others in court; furthermore, apart from the Lancashire and Durham courts, chancery judges sit exclusively in London and do not go on circuit. They sit in the Royal Courts of Justice in the Strand. Juries are not used in Chancery Division because of its historical development.

For an outline of civil court procedure see page 96.

PROBATE, DIVORCE AND ADMIRALTY DIVISION OF THE HIGH COURT

This division, sometimes fondly known as the Wills, Wives and Wrecks Division, is—as will be shown in the following pages—the subject of proposals for radical change. The Lord Chancellor, in consultation with the Bar Council and the Law Society, put forward proposals in 1969 under which Divorce and Admiralty would each be a separate division and Probate would be merged with Chancery. The name of the Divorce Division would be changed to Family Division and would take over the work concerning infants which is, at present, the task of Chancery Division.

Probate

In ancient times the king could seize the goods of persons who died intestate. This power was granted as a franchise to the lords of the manor and to persons of similar standing, and to the church. The thirty-second article of Magna Carta (1215) guarded against misuse of this power but even so, there was still wide abuse. The Statute of Westminster II (1285) said that the Ordinary, ie the ecclesiastical judges, were bound to pay the debts of the intestate person so far as the goods would allow. The abuses continued and in 1357 Edward III said that the Ordinaries 'shall depute the next and most lawful friends of the dead person intestate to administer his goods'. In 1529, Henry VIII gave the ecclesiastical judges power to grant administration either to the widow or to the next-of-kin, or even to both, at the judge's discretion. Finally on 1 January 1858 this jurisdiction was transferred to the Court of Probate under one judge, with a right of appeal to the House of Lords.

All people die testate or intestate. Testate means they leave a will; intestate means they do not. It does not matter whether a will is home-made, or drawn up before a qualified lawyer; it is equally valid, provided it is properly executed and attested. Even so, the Probate Court may be involved in the affairs of a deceased person whether or not there is a will. The majority of wills are not disputed, but occasionally conflict does arise.

An executor, named in a will, may wish to be absolved from his duties. He can do this by renunciation, or the other executors can obtain a Grant of Probate with power reserved to the executor who does not wish to prove. If this method is followed, the executor who wishes to renounce can later take up his duties if he changes his mind. Grant of probate means legal authentication of the effectiveness of the will and, to obtain this, application must be made to the Principal Probate Registry at Somerset House, or to a District Probate Registry. If there is a possibility of death duties, the estate will have to be valued and the duty paid before any grant of probate is made.

Anyone who disputes the validity of a will, or who claims

benefit from a later will or codicil, may lodge a *caveat* at the registry. The words mean 'let him beware'; so a *caveat* is an intimation made to the proper officer of a court to prevent the taking of any step without intimation to the party interested to appear. This results in a contentious procedure being observed with later proceedings in the Probate Division of the High Court. The word contentious means legal business where there is a contest. The majority of properly drawn-up wills include an attestation clause. This throws the burden of proof on to those who seek to show it was not properly executed. Without this clause, the will must be proved by sworn witnesses.

When the Registry grants probate, the probate order is issued and the executor assumes, usually from the will itself, all title to the testator's property. He must pay all debts and share the remainder between the beneficiaries. Questions of administration may be heard by the Chancery Division and not by the Probate Division. If a person dies intestate, an administrator must be appointed. He must enter into bonds for the proper administration because he was not chosen by the deceased for this task. He must pay all debts and expenses, and has very wide powers. He may even sell objects although he should not dispose of a widow's or family's home. He may deal informally with certain things, but never with land. Every so often a will does not provide for a family; in these cases, application for maintenance can be made to Chancery Division.

As already mentioned, it is seldom that a probate case reaches court. If it does, the trial may be in the High Court, although it can be heard either at the assizes or a county court. In disputed cases, the proceedings are similar to those of Queen's Bench Division.

Probate has survived because of the ecclesiastical courts—even in the Middle Ages the administration of wills was done by them. Earlier than the twelfth century, the ecclesiastics taught that a man's soul would benefit by his giving his worldly wealth to the Church; if therefore a man omitted to decide the fate of his property, the Church would decide for him. This became ingrained in the faithful to such a degree that, even if a will was made, the bishop's court would make sure it was proven before the trustees executed the wishes of the dead person. If a person died intestate, the disposal of his goods was left to the Church, in the shape of the bishop and his court.

Before the Probate Court was established, the Dean of Arches in Canterbury Province, who sat in St Mary-le-Bow Church, dealt with this type of work. There is now a strong feeling that probate work should be dealt with by Chancery because it is so similar.

Divorce

One of the first recorded divorces among the Romans occurred in 331 BC, although it was apparently permitted by the Mosaic law as long ago as 1451 BC. After this particular Roman divorce, however, it became commonplace in spite of preventive measures in the shape of laws such as the *Lex de maritandis ordinibus* passed in 18 BC, and the *Lex Pappia-Poppoea* in AD 9. Early divorces were in fact permitted by canon law which specified reasons including spiritual impediments to marriage such as consanguinity, affinity within the forbidden degrees, impotence, adultery, etc.

In England it was the formation of the divorce courts which brought to an end the jurisdiction of the ecclesiastical courts over matrimonial affairs. Ecclesiastical courts had long exercised a firm hold over the legal and religious life of the country, and also exercised jurisdiction over wills, intestacies and all probate matters. This came to an end with the passing of a Divorce and Matrimonial Causes Act 1857.

Martin Luther is said to have introduced civil marriage by saying 'Marriage is a worldly thing'. Civil marriage, as opposed to spiritual matrimony was established in 1653 but divorce, as a totally civil rather than spiritual matter, had not yet arrived. This did not happen until 1857. In England the early divorces were of two kinds:

A mensa et thoro	Here the parties lived apart (literal meaning: from table and bed), but the marriage vows were not dissolved.
A vinculo matrimonii	literal meaning: from the bond of matrimony). This meant the union was illegal from the start. The marriage was subsequently dissolved.

The first divorce to succeed without the consent of a spiritual court, was that of the Countess of Macclesfield on 2 April 1698, and this was the first weakening of the power of the ecclesiastical courts.

The making of divorce legislation has always been difficult —and still is. In 1798, Lord Loughborough secured the approval of a series of resolutions which required every applicant for divorce to be supported by ecclesiastical sentence and by a previous verdict at law. Prior to 1840, divorce bills in the commons were decided by the entire House; in that year they were referred to a nine-man committee.

The next development was in December 1850 when commissioners were appointed to enquire into the divorce laws. The final separation from the ecclesiastical courts came in 1857: their authority over divorce was abolished and placed with the Court for Divorce and Matrimonial Causes. This was presided over by three judges, one of whom was a Probate judge. Even though the Divorce Court could grant decrees, the cost was prohibitive, but the introduction of Legal Aid in 1949 brought it within the scope of most people.

As already mentioned, it has been suggested that this part of the Probate, Divorce and Admiralty Division of the High Court be re-formed as the Family Division, which would have the current matrimonial jurisdiction of the present Probate, Divorce and Admiralty. Its work would also include the wardship, adoption and guardianship of infants which is currently done by Chancery Division, although there would be an interchange on this type of case between the Family Division and Chancery.

Procedure

Divorce proceedings begin with the filing of a petition by the person requiring the divorce. It must give details of the alleged matrimonial offence and upon this the request for the divorce is based. This document is placed in the Divorce Registry in London, or with a county court registrar if the county court in question has been designated as a Divorce County Court. He may act as District Registrar of the High Court in places outside London but in all cases the procedure is the same.

If the respondent wishes to contest the action, he must file his answer at the Divorce County Court; he must be served with a notice of the petition against him and this can be done either personally or by post. If an answer is filed the Registrar must, in nearly all cases, order the cause to be transferred to the High Court. A respondent can cross-petition. This must be filed within a reasonable time of the alleged matrimonial offence but cannot be done within three years of marriage except in cases of hardship. When the registrar certifies that a case is ready for trial, he will decide upon the venue and mode of trial. All parties will be informed and the case can be heard.

A divorce case may be heard by a judge of the Divorce Division, either in London or in the assize courts. Several High Court judges are assigned to the Divorce Division. In practice, only the long, defended cases are heard at the assizes and they are not heard at the same time as the criminal and civil lists. Separate days are set aside. A short defended case can be tried by special commissioners of divorce who include all county court judges. They try divorces in selected towns and have all the powers of a High Court judge. Undefended divorces are now heard in the Divorce County Courts by the judge of that county court sitting in his capacity as a county court judge. The commissioners hear their cases in the buildings used as county courts (which can also be used as magistrates' courts), and sometimes in the assize courts. Unless the case has special nullity grounds, it is tried in open court although the activities of the press are restricted. They can print the charges, the findings and the judgement, but not the evidence. The examination of witnesses and the order of speeches follows the pattern of that in the Queen's Bench Division although the respondent is not bound to give evidence. Persons cited as co-respondents may be separately represented by counsel.

If a judge finds a case proven he will first announce a *decree nisi* in favour of the petitioner; three months later the decree may become absolute although in special circumstances this period can be shortened. Secondary considerations must be heeded by a divorce judge. These include the custody of children and the financial arrangements for the wife and family. No decree absolute can be made until the judge has certified his satisfaction with the arrangements for the children and the family. Details of such arrangements must be given in the petition. There is right of appeal to the Court of Appeal if a decree is granted or refused.

Undefended suits, which take a matter of minutes to decide, form a large proportion of divorce cases. Even in these, which arise when neither partner wishes to save the marriage, the basic procedure is followed. In these cases, the petition is served on the respondent and any co-respondents. They can make written confessions but in court any spouse who does not attend must be formally identified. This can be done through an enquiry agent if necessary, who may have taken statements for the proceedings. As with defended cases, the court must grant a *decree nisi* and make the necessary orders for custody of children, etc.

The grounds for divorce are at present:

   (i) Adultery
  (ii) Desertion
 (iii) Cruelty
 (iv) Five years' continuous and incurable insanity
  (v) Offences of rape, sodomy or bestiality committed by a husband since marriage.

The following is a brief outline of the new grounds which will become effective when the Divorce Reform Act 1969 comes into force on 1 January 1971. Under the 1969 Act, the sole ground on which a petition for divorce may be presented to the court by either party to a marriage, shall be that the marriage has broken down irretrievably.

However, to satisfy a court that a marriage has broken down 'irretrievably', the petitioner must prove one of the following points:

(i) That the respondent has committed adultery and the petitioner finds it intolerable to live with him (or her)
(ii) That the respondent has behaved in such a way that the petitioner cannot reasonably be expected to live with him (or her)
(iii) That the respondent has deserted the petitioner for a continuous period of at least two years (immediately preceding the presentation of the petition)
(iv) That the parties have lived apart for a continuous period of at least two years (immediately preceding the presentation of the petition) *and* the respondent consents to a decree being granted
(v) That the parties have lived apart for a continuous period of at least five years (immediately preceding the presentation of the petition).

A husband and wife shall be treated as living apart unless they are living with each other in the same household.

These new grounds provide, for the first time, that spouses may lawfully agree to be separated with a view to a subsequent divorce, and collusion is no longer a bar. It permits divorce if they have lived apart and both consent to the decree (item (iv) above), and it also enables a petitioner to seek divorce after five years separation whether or not the other party consents, and irrespective of whether the petitioner deserted the other spouse or was deserted. Each of the above is regarded as evidence of the irretrievable breakdown of a marriage; from this the court will decide whether or not the union has completely broken down.

This will make divorce much easier, although section 3 of the new Act is designed to encourage reconciliation where possible. The petitioner's solicitor must certify whether he has discussed reconciliation with the petitioner, and he must supply the names and addresses of qualified persons who might assist in this, eg welfare officers, clergymen, marriage guidance councillors, etc, and the court can adjourn the proceedings if there is a possibility of reconciliation.

Admiralty

The origins of the Admiralty Court are uncertain. Some historians suggest it was created by Edward III, while others are positive it existed much earlier. Under Richard II it was divided into the Instance Court and the Prize Court, and as such was held at Orton Quay near London Bridge, but later transferred to Doctor's Commons.

In those early days, the judge was the deputy of the Lord High Admiral and the supervision of naval matters was entrusted to him. At that time, the court, known as the High Court of Admiralty, held both criminal and civil jurisdiction but later its criminal jurisdiction was transferred (see page 27).

Reports of an Admiralty court go back to 1357 although many other courts had admiralty jurisdiction. Local courts, such as the seaport courts of Ipswich and Padstow and those of the Cinque ports are good examples. Their hearings were held in all manner of odd places—on board ship, in various buildings and even on the open shore! Their haphazard nature led Edward III (1327-77) to institute a more formal type of admiralty court. One story says that, due to a local court's decision, he had to pay out of his own pocket in 1337 for damage to a Genoese ship! He therefore decided to put things right and his opportunity came in 1340 when the Battle of Sluys gave him supremacy at sea. He called himself Sovereign of the Seas and founded his Admiralty court to maintain both his sovereignty and the king's peace on the high seas. Apart from the local courts, other Admiralty matters had previously been heard in the common law courts, or perhaps before the Lord Chancellor or even the King's Council.

Richard II (1377-99) defined the jurisdiction of the Admiralty court by saying it must not deal with matters of contract, pleas, quarrels and similar matters which arose on land. It could deal with deaths or maiming on ships in the rivers, or beneath bridges at the river's mouth. The first judge of the Admiralty court was appointed in 1482 and during those formative years there was a lot of bickering between the common law courts and Admiralty as to their precise jurisdiction. The result was that Admiralty lost some of its powers. Later, even more jurisdiction was removed during the Long Parliament.

Until 1536 it had jurisdiction over all crime committed at sea by His Majesty's subjects, or by crews of British ships. In that year, jurisdiction over this sort of crime went to the common law courts where it remained until 1834. In that year, maritime crimes became the prerogative of the Central Criminal Court in London (the Old Bailey) and they remain there to this day.

In 1840, however, the first Admiralty Courts Acts were passed to give increased jurisdiction to the court so that it could try civil cases. It was also given power to enforce its orders. All other maritime courts were abolished by the Municipal Corporation Act 1835, and the Merchant Shipping Acts gave the Admiralty Court its present jurisdiction.

The possibility of a merger, as a matter of convenience to High Court business, between the Probate Court and the High Court of Admiralty came in 1857. It was then statutorily provided that the next vacancy for a judge in the Admiralty Court could be filled by a judge of the Probate Court. Alternatively, if the vacancy appeared in the Probate Court, it could be filled by an Admiralty judge. The actual merger was brought about by the Judicature Act of 1873 which instituted the division of the High Court known as Probate, Divorce and Admiralty Division. Its home is in the Strand, in the Law Courts, and seamen from all over the world bring actions here. Admiralty courts are recognised by the symbolic anchor above the head of the court's president.

Procedure

The proceedings in the Admiralty court are broadly similar to the usual civil court procedure, but differ because it is an international court which tries cases involving foreign vessels. Furthermore, there is no jury.

If a judge requires nautical advice he can request the help of a nautical assessor, but usually two Elder Brethren of Trinity House sit in court to advise him. These are retired high ranking naval officers—members of the royal family may even be included. They only decide points involving maritime custom and ritual; the judge decides points of law.

Just as there are winds of change in the assizes, quarter sessions and the divorce and probate courts, so there is also a movement to amend, albeit slightly, the functions of Admiralty Division. The proposals are that it forms a new Admiralty and Commercial Court, within Queen's Bench Division, but with the same jurisdiction as the Admiralty Court of today. It has been suggested that the judges of the new court be allowed to sit in private if necessary, without robes, and also to dispense with the rules of evidence.

CIVIL COURT PROCEDURE

Pleadings

Civil court procedure varies so much that it is not possible to deal explicitly with every type within these pages. A general outline only is therefore given. Where civil proceedings are contemplated, the solicitors who represent the parties will usually work towards a settlement out of court. If this fails they will resort to civil action in the courts.

When an action is destined for any court of the Queen's Bench Division it will start with the issue of a writ, on which a statement of claim is sometimes endorsed. This is the first step, and the name of this document may vary according to the court which will try the case. The nature of the dispute will be set out in the writ and the defendant must be notified of this. If he wishes to contest the action, the appropriate forms are completed and this is known as 'entering an appearance'. It should be done within eight days.

When this has been done, the plaintiff must next deliver his 'statement of claim'. This must contain all the material facts to support his action, for the defendant must know the basis of the claim although there is no need to inform him of the evidence to be used. The compilation of these documents is governed by rules, any breach of which may result in an application from the defendant to have the statement 'struck out'. If this is successful, it means that the plaintiff must provide a new statement of claim. The defendant can then ask for more details to support the allegations against him.

Upon receipt of the statement of claim, the defendant must give his version of the affair and this is done in a document called a 'defence'. It gives his side of the story and lists facts to support it. Any denials of fact which are quoted in the opponent's statement of claim must be included, together with any new facts.

The next document which may be used is called a 'reply'. This is for further allegations by a plaintiff which arise when he reads the defence, and this see-saw procedure may continue until each party has covered and dealt with every relevant fact. Generally, it is necessary only to submit the statement of claim and the defence which answers to it.

Occasions do arise, however, when a defendant alleges that a plaintiff's claim is totally unfounded. He may even allege that he himself has a just claim against the other party and in these cases, a counter-claim is made. This is in effect a statement of claim used in reverse of the general method—a reply to this is called a 'defence to counter-claim'.

Collectively speaking, all these documents are known as 'pleadings'. When each side ceases to plead any further fact, the pleadings are said to be closed. A summons is issued for directions of trial and this is heard by a Registrar if the proceedings are in a District Registry of the High Court outside London, or by a Master in London.

Pleadings are framed in every-day language instead of legal jargon, but they are carefully drafted by counsel. A complete

G

list of all the documentary evidence from both sides must be made and an oath is taken that the lists are complete.

Other preliminaries before trial

Each side must allow his documentary evidence to be inspected by his opponents, so that each has all the documentary evidence to hand. From this, a case can be prepared. Solicitors may seek counsel's advice at this stage and, for civil proceedings, this is perhaps the most important part. From this documentary evidence the case is made out.

Each side may also put questions to the other and these must be answered on oath. The answers may be read at a subsequent hearing and are known as 'interrogatories'. This questioning, which is still out of court, is used only to establish facts which are suspected by one side, and only in the absence of relevant documentary evidence. All this is done before the case reaches court.

Nor do the preliminaries end there. There may be more documentary work involving such forms as the 'Notice to Produce', a document which has to be inspected by either party, or there may be a 'Notice to Admit' in which one party may admit all the facts not in dispute, but at the same time may not admit liability. There is now a similar provision in the criminal courts, which is known as 'Proof by formal admission'. This was introduced by the Criminal Justice Act 1967 and the idea is that a person may admit part of a case against him, and yet plead not guilty. (For example, he may admit driving a car which killed a person and yet plead not guilty to causing the man's death by dangerous driving).

In a civil case, inspection of documents is done as follows. If a Notice to Produce is given by either party to the other this requires the receiving party to produce originals of documents in court. However, provided a Notice to Produce has been given, the party giving it may produce a *copy* of the original document in evidence. If a Notice to Produce is not given, a copy may not be given in evidence because it is not the best evidence. The 'best evidence' means the original. Where there has been correspondence between the parties, each will give to the other Notice to Produce the original letters. This then enables the parties to produce in evidence the carbon copy of the original. A Notice to Admit is given by one party to the other. If the latter admits a fact or facts in respect of which Notice to Admit has been given, then no further proof is necessary. If he does not admit the fact then the party giving Notice to Admit must make formal proof of the fact or facts at the hearing. If, however, the court considers that they ought to have been admitted, then the party failing to admit the fact may be condemned in the additional costs incurred in proving that fact.

When all the necessary documentation is complete, the case is set down for trial. This stage of an action might arrive after some considerable delay—it is this aspect of the judicial system which so often gives rise to complaint.

Dates, times, venues and other details of the hearing are given to all concerned, including witnesses. If a witness refuses to attend, a subpoena will be issued to compel his attendance and his giving evidence. The word means 'under penalty'—to ignore a subpoena is regarded as contempt of court and it carries heavy penalties in both civil and criminal courts. In practice, many voluntary witnesses are subpoenaed to ensure their attendance. A last-minute change of mind by a voluntary witness could lead to an adjournment, which is costly and time-wasting.

It often happens that civil matters are settled out of court even at this late stage, but in the event of a case reaching the stage where it must appear before the court, the procedure follows a fairly standard pattern.

The trial
Proceedings are started by counsel for the plaintiff. He out-lines the matters in dispute and the judge listens. There may, on some occasions, be a jury who must also listen. Their func-tions and selection are almost identical to those shown in chapter two (page 36).
Counsel then reads the pleadings to the court and puts for-

ward his client's arguments. He emphasises the facts which support his case. The first witness is called by him. This person takes the oath or makes a solemn declaration or affirmation and is examined on his evidence by questions from counsel. As in a criminal court, the rules of evidence apply in that certain questions, eg leading questions, cannot usually be asked, nor can hearsay evidence be admitted except in certain circumstances permitted by the Civil Evidence Act of 1968.

When the plaintiff's counsel has concluded his questioning of a witness, known as the examination-in-chief, counsel for the defendant will then put questions to this witness. This is known as cross-examination and is used in an effort to discredit the witness's story. Leading questions can be asked during a cross-examination, just as they are in criminal proceedings.

After the cross-examination, the plaintiff's counsel may re-examine this same witness, but only on matters arising from the cross-examination.

After the witness has been thoroughly examined, he leaves the box and the next witness goes through the same procedure. The hearing continues until all the plaintiff's witnesses have given evidence. It is now the turn of the defendant.

At this stage, there may be a submission that the evidence does not support the plaintiff's claim. If the judge agrees, the case may end and the defendant will be discharged. Otherwise it will continue and it is the turn of the defendant to produce his witnesses. They will be brought into the witness box to be sworn, then examined, cross-examined and re-examined by counsel.

When each has given evidence, counsel for the defendant will deliver a speech showing how the plaintiff has failed to establish a case. When this speech is over, the plaintiff's counsel will give his version and it is after these speeches that the judge will consider judgement.

If there is a jury, the judge will explain their duty to them and he may assist on points of law. He may clarify the facts which they are to determine and may refresh them on issues raised. The decision is theirs and theirs alone. When a judge sits without a jury, the decision rests upon him and he will deliver it in court. There is always right of appeal against a decision and this lies to the Court of Appeal (Civil Division).

This account is necessarily short; serious students are recommended to read either Kiralfy or Lewis.

FIVE
Coroners

Although the coroner is one of England's oldest public officials, it frequently happens that he has no court room of his own. He must often be content with any suitable accommodation; this might be an existing court house, a room in a town hall or an office in a police station, but an inquest must never be held in a public house if other premises are available. A coroner is further restricted in that he must not hold inquests on a Sunday, nor normally on Good Friday, Christmas Day or a bank holiday.

Currently there are between 200 and 300 coroners in England and Wales of whom about 15 are full-time. Full-time coroners are found in London and some other larger cities and usually possess both legal and medical qualifications. Scotland does not have a coroner—the equivalent office is that of Procurator Fiscal.

Coroners are generally chosen from practising solicitors who work part-time at their coroner's duties and the main qualification for appointment is to be either a barrister, a solicitor or registered medical practitioner of not less than five years standing. These qualifications also apply to deputy coroners. Some persons are coroners by virtue of their office—the Lord Chief Justice of England is the supreme coroner for England, and all the judges of the High Court of Justice are sovereign coroners for the whole of England. The majority are appointed by their respective local authority but are regarded as holding office under the Crown. Their full title is Her Majesty's Coroner.

The chief duties of a coroner are:

(i) To enquire into the death, in particular the cause of
   death, of certain persons either by holding an inquest
   or by ordering a post mortem examination
(ii) To hold inquests on treasure trove.

In the City of London the coroners' duties include the holding
of inquests on outbreaks of fire.
   To understand the reasons for this unique and ancient office,
it is necessary to learn something of its origins.

HISTORY

It is difficult to date the origins of the office of coroner with
any accuracy. The generally accepted date is 1194, although
it is probable that persons with similar duties existed long
before, perhaps in Saxon times. In 1194 though there is reference to the coroner in the Articles of Eyre, which set out
the eyre of the king's justices of September of that year under
Richard I, and provided also for the election of three knights
and one clerk in each county. They were to be custodians of
the pleas of the Crown. The clerk was usually an ecclesiastic
who had to assist the coroner or even act as his deputy during
inquests. Many legal historians therefore regard 1194 as the
true beginning of the office of coroner. The position seems to
have arisen in an effort to curtail the activities of an even
more ancient office—that of sheriff. Many early sheriffs abused
their powers and so the coroner became, among other things,
their watchdog.
   The name coroner may have come from the French *corune*
or *coroune*, meaning a crown. In the Articles of Eyre there
appears the phrase *custos placitorum coronae* which means
'the guardian of the pleas of the Crown'. In the twelfth century, the coroner was known as *Serviens Regis*, or sometimes
Serviens Hundred, a name which was given to him in the pipe
rolls of Richard I and Henry II. Later, in 1204, the word
coronarius appears; it is also to be found in Magna Carta. The
Anglo-French word *coruner* is used in the second statute of
Edward I in 1275 and appears again in 1292 when describing

the office of coroner of the king's household. It seems that the English word coroner or crowner first appeared during the fourteenth century. The latter was recently in use in Northern Ireland and is sometimes used as a slang term in the north of England.

Because he was keeper of the king's pleas, the early coroner had to 'keep pleas, suits or causes which affected the King's crown and dignity'. The precise interpretation of this was usually decided by the king himself, or by someone acting on his behalf. The coroner's role, therefore, was mainly clerical and not supervisory. He had to ensure that all chance revenues, consisting mainly of paid fines, were paid to His Majesty: a coroner kept a record of all crimes so that he could gather the money for the king. His duties also consisted of the supervision of income from the forfeited chattels of felons; and from deodands, wrecks, royal fish and treasure trove. These items were also known as chance revenues and were payable to the Crown; the coroner had to make sure this was done. This type of case was heard in the City of London by the sheriffs and the coroners, but later the coroners travelled the country to perform their duties.

In addition to this administrative work, he did hold inquests on deaths which had occurred due to violence, accident or in prison. He looked into accusations of felony and committed suspects for trial. When the early coroner heard a case he was assisted by a jury and his enquiry was called an *inquisitio*. The word inquest or inquisition is derived from this.

His role as clerk disappeared when a famous statute was passed in 1276; this was *De Officia Coronatoris*, since repealed. It laid down that:

A coroner should go to the place where any person is slain or suddenly dead or wounded, or where houses are broken, or where treasure is to be found, and should by his warrant to the bailiffs or constables summon a jury out of four or five neighbouring towns to make enquiry upon view of the body; and the coroner and the jury should enquire into the manner of the killing.

The coroner had to view the body (and in fact still does) and had to look for signs of strangulation, burns or wounds. Furthermore he had to examine weapons and take down evidence of witnesses in writing. He had the power to commit to prison any person found guilty by his inquisition and this power persists today, in a slightly amended form. When a coroner committed anyone to prison for trial at the assizes, all the inquest witnesses were bound over to appear too, to give their evidence.

Even in medieval times, the investigation of sudden or unexplained death was regarded as important, but for reasons other than those existing today. The motive was then a financial one. Punitive systems were used to ensure notification to the coroner of such deaths. One method involved fines and was probably introduced by William the Conqueror to prevent the secret murder of his Norman soldiers by the Saxons. The fine was forty-six marks—very high in those times—and it was levied on the lord of the district in which a Norman's body was found. If the killer was traced within five days, the fine was not paid. But the lords were cunning because they passed the burden of this fine to the villagers and declared that all bodies were Norman unless proved otherwise. So the lord indemnified themselves and also gathered in useful sums from the unfortunate peasants because conclusive proof that a body was not a Norman was so difficult to obtain. This became vitally important to the early inquests and became known as 'proof of englishry'; it existed until 1340.

The duty of the early coroners was to decide the responsibility of persons who committed wilful murder, as opposed to deaths by accident, self-defence or simple negligence. Forfeiture of property was the punishment for a convicted felon; an accident, irrespective of the seriousness of its consequences, could never be a felony and forfeiture could not apply. The coroner had to decide if felony had been committed and, if so, he had to supervise forfeiture of the felon's goods.

We have mentioned 'deodand'; this was the actual object responsible for a death. It might be a knife, a cart or anything. Whatever it was, it had to be handed to the Crown and this was one of the chance revenues to be supervised by the coroner. A good example occurred in 1227 when a man was killed by a cart. It was drawn by two horses and there was a pig on board at the time. The whole lot—cart, horse and pig—was valued at 6s (30p) and declared deodand. Maybe this was unusual—normally it was the wheel of a cart which had killed a man which was declared deodand, rather than the entire vehicle.

Occasionally the Crown would renounce its right to a deodand and would award it, or the equivalent value, to the deceased's relatives. But the lords of the times stepped in. They obtained the post of foreman of any coroner's jury where a valuable deodand was at stake and got it for themselves.

The deodand system continued into fairly modern times—there are instances of ships and carriages being declared deodand, sometimes involving huge sums of money. As late as 1841 the Registrar General said the system was a wise one, but it was abolished by Queen Victoria in 1846 because it was feared that entire railway trains would be declared deodand and forfeited. With the deodand's disappearance, another of the coroner's more curious duties was removed.

Another obsolete duty was listing outlaws and holding an inquest on their belongings which were forfeited to the Crown. The sheriff was the man who declared a man an outlaw—he still had this power as late as 1938 and could even summon a posse! A coroner also abjured felons who fled to sanctuary. A sanctuary could be almost anywhere—a church, school, hospital, an open space or even a mint. They had one thing in common—they were owned by the Church.

The custom of keeping places to which a criminal could flee to sanctuary is difficult to date, but in AD 887 King Alfred the Great allowed him to obtain safety in a church for three days. By common law this was extended to thirty days, but a fleeing man was bound to confess his crimes when in sanctuary. He swore before the archbishop's bailiff that he would be faithful to the spiritual authorities, as well as to the bailiff, governors, burgesses and commoners of the town. He also swore that he would 'bere no poynted wepen, dagger or knyfe, ne none other wepen against the king's peace'; that he would assist in quelling strife and extinguishing fire, and that he would be ready for such action at the warning of the 'belman'. If his place of sanctuary was a church, he swore in addition that he would 'do his dewte in syngyng and offer at the masse on the morne'. It was so easy to break sanctuary—a criminal could creep away at night and escape; but if the sanctuary was a church the brethren had to protect, feed and entertain the felon for thirty days!

A felon in sanctuary was not completely free from the law because he could remain there for only thirty days. After that time he expected to be punished, although one avenue was open to him. This is where the coroner enters the system.

A person in sanctuary was taken before the coroner to confess his crimes and abjure the realm. To abjure was to swear on oath to leave the realm for ever and, when this was done, the felon was branded on the flesh of his thumb with the letter A (meaning abjured). Everyone then knew of his misdeeds. The coroner next named a port to which the felon had to travel as quickly as possible in the appropriate manner, ie barefoot, bare-headed and carrying a cross. Any deviation from his route made him liable to be killed by the locals. At the port, he had to catch the first departing ship; if there was no ship, he had to wade into the sea every day to show his endeavour to leave. A lot of felons thought this was better than being hanged but in practice, very few ever reached the shore; they became outlaws instead. When a person abjured the realm, or became an outlaw, his property was forfeited to the Crown, but the system was a poor one and ended in 1540. A few places of sanctuary did remain until 1624 when they were finally abolished. And when this was done, another of the coroner's tasks vanished.

A threat to the coroner arose in the fourteenth century when the newly formed justices of the peace began to conduct preliminary investigations of persons suspected of homicide with the result that they eventually gained a measure of control over the coroners. By the end of the fifteenth century, coroners ceased to be of any real importance in the general judicial system.

Then, after over two centuries of suppression, came a suggestion of reform. An Act of Parliament in 1751 provided payment to coroners for all inquests held by them, and it authorised travelling expenses of 9d (4p) a mile. The Act was designed to encourage the holding of inquests in *all* cases of sudden and unexpected death, and not restrict them to persons who had been slain. The fee was 20s (£1) per inquest, plus an additional 13s 4d (66½p) for slain persons. The fees came out of the rates. Payment of such fees, however, depended upon their approval by the justices who had controlled the coroners since the fourteenth century and their tight-fisted interpretation of the relevant statutes created havoc with the coroners' work. An example was the delayed introduction of medical evidence at inquests which in turn meant that murder was often hidden. By restricting expenditure of public money, the justices were allowing murderers to escape.

In 1819 a committee said that, in this country no atrocious crime could remain secret, so the coroner again met trouble over his power to hold inquests in all cases of sudden death. One judge advocated inquests only when violence could be seen on a body; another felt that drowned bodies should be buried without an inquest; yet another felt that inquests should be held only when the coroner was called by the proper officials and only then if there was no doubt about the manner of death.

There arose around this period the eternal question about the merits of coroners but in spite of this, legislation was introduced in 1836 for the payment of medical witnesses at inquests. It also introduced payment for post mortem examinations and for other medical investigations. The coroner was given power to demand such examinations; in addition he could order the person carrying out the medical examination to be a witness at his inquest. Medical evidence was therefore introduced officially into the coroner's inquest—a vital and long-overdue step in legal procedure. And yet the justices still refused to allow payments of fees for deaths when there was no evidence of criminal violence. Later they even prevented coroners being told of sudden deaths.

If it is remembered at this stage that the origin of the coroner was to ensure that monies were paid to the Crown, then it seems the justices and even the judges of the last century were still thinking along those lines. They missed the real value of the inquest. For many years the judiciary believed that the coroner only had jurisdiction over bodies which had met violent or unmistakenly unnatural death. They ignored poisons and drownings, consequently they ignored murder. This is still evident in some of the coroner's nineteenth-century duties, eg in 1843 they still held inquests on the chattels of convicted felons and it was not until 1826 that the enquiry into the goods and lands of fugitives ceased. As late as 1854, a coroner could seize the goods of fugitives on behalf of the sovereign or his almoners.

A step forward came in 1836 when the Births and Deaths Registration Act came into force, ordering the nation-wide registration of these events. The Act said that a body could not be buried without either a certificate from the registrar, or a coroner's order. This resulted in a vast increase in deaths reported to the coroner. The justices still argued about who should pay the expenses, but the value of the coroner's inquest was beginning to prove itself.

In 1845 the Home Secretary explained to the House of Commons how one murderer had disposed of twenty victims without any inquest being held and, about the same time, the newspapers began to agitate about the interference of the justices. The Times of 13 June 1846 said that coroners should be allowed to continue their ancient office and the public were solidly in agreement. Even so, the justices still said that coroners were too ready to spend money and, because of this, inquests were being held as late as 1850 without medical evidence.

At this time, the police force, then a new institution, became involved in the conflict between coroners and justices. In 1857, the Chief Constable of the East Riding Constabulary ordered that the coroner must not be called if a death was accidental, such as from falling off a horse, or from a building or scaffolding, or if it concerned a baby overlaid in bed. The police in general took little official interest in sudden deaths at that time, but attacks from other quarters were being directed at the justices. In 1858, for example, the Registrar General criticised them for their stupidity and gave instances where murder had not been found through lack of medical evidence at inquests. Such cases arose when burial clubs were popular, for they provided the contributing parents with ready cash when their children died. The police did not see any connection between this and reports of children being overlaid in bed. In the meantime, a Mr William Payne was working on behalf of his fellow coroners. In 1846, in spite of tremendous opposition, he founded the Coroners Society which in 1860 managed to win the appointment of coroners on a salaried basis. They became quite independent of the justices.

In 1859, a Royal Commission said that inquests should be held in all cases of accidental or sudden death, and it further recommended that the duty of notifying coroners should rest with the police. It was felt better to hold a few unnecessary inquests rather than leave serious crimes undetected, and it was recommended in 1860 that inquests be held in every case of violent or unnatural death. A Select Committee on Coroners went even further to say that inquests should be held where death was the result of an unknown cause, which included instances where death seemed to be from natural causes, but where there was any suggestion of a criminal act. This was the major break-through. These recommendation were approved in the Coroners Act 1887 which formed, and still forms, the basis of their duties. The justices were wholeheartedly condemned for their past interference and the numbers of inquests rose steeply. So did the numbers of coroners' committals for trial of persons charged with murder.

One of the provisions of the Act was not vastly different from a clause contained in the statute of 1340, ie that candidates for the office of coroner must own land. The result was that prospective coroners bought land to become eligible—

some even bought grave plots! This persisted until 1926 when this qualification was scrapped.

Another oddity about the 1887 Act was that it still allowed the justices to exercise control over the coroners, through payment of their fees. But now, still smarting after severe criticism, they became more helpful, and in 1888 coroners were freed from their supervision. Today their remuneration and expenses are the responsibility of the local authority which appoints them.

INFORMING THE CORONER

A coroner must hold an inquest in all cases where he is informed that the dead body of a person is lying in his jurisdiction *and* where he has reasonable cause to suspect violent or unnatural death, or death from some unknown cause, or if that person has died in prison, or in such a place or in circumstances where an inquest is required by an Act of Parliament.

The term 'body' in this connection, has never been defined. It might not include a non-viable foetus because this is a human being at a very early stage of development and incapable of having a separate existence. This being so, it is legally incapable of living and therefore incapable of dying, but a coroner would no doubt make initial enquiries if such an occasion arose. The same applies to a still-born child. Parts of a body, or even bones from only part of a body, are regarded as bodies for the purpose of inquests and coroners can hold inquests upon such discoveries. An inquest cannot be held on persons who, if alive, would have been entitled to diplomatic privilege unless privilege is not claimed, or if the Home Secretary, upon being consulted, advises the holding of an inquest.

In order to hold an inquest, a coroner has the common law power to order exhumation of a body which is buried within his jurisdiction. He can do this without consulting the Home Office although in practice this is always done. The 1887 Act did not impose a duty to report all deaths to the coroner as it was felt there was a common law duty to do this; it is now statutorily provided for. The police act as coroners' officers in the majority of cases and notify the coroner of all sudden deaths. They also make the necessary enquiries on behalf of the coroner.

In some forces the first policeman at the scene is thereupon the coroner's officer for that particular death. This can result in, say, a nineteen-year-old constable suddenly finding himself dealing with a sudden death, whether it be murder, accident or suicide. On the other hand, the police officer in question might have many years experience in criminal investigation work. But irrespective of that experience, he is responsible for enquiries into the death and he arranges the post mortem, the inquest and other necessities. In some small forces, or in the larger police divisions, a police officer is specially appointed to act as coroner's officer. He deals with all sudden deaths; these men are usually sergeants or inspectors and it is their full-time job.

More often than not, an unexplained, unnatural, sudden or accidental death first comes to the notice of the police. Old people who die alone, road accidents or industrial accidents, murders, suicides and simple sudden deaths are reported to them as a matter of course and this sets in motion the wheels which lead via the post mortem to the inquest.

As well as being told by the police, the coroner may also be informed by doctors who cannot certify the cause of death, and a similar duty binds registrars of births and deaths. They must notify the coroner when it appears the deceased has not been seen by a doctor either within the fourteen days prior to death, or after death. Rather oddly, there is no legal duty upon doctors to view a body before certifying the reason for its death. Harvard estimates that, every year, over 100,000 persons are certified dead without being seen by a doctor and tells of a man who was shot through the heart but who was certified as having died through heart attack! Another instance involved a woman who had suffered a long illness, she was certified as having died through that illness where in fact she had been strangled.

BEFORE THE INQUEST

When a coroner is thus notified of a death, he must first decide whether he has jurisdiction over the body, ie whether it is within his area. It is immaterial where the *cause* of death arose, or even where death occurred. The important point is where the body is now lying and it is the responsibility of the coroner in whose area it happens to be. He has no jurisdiction over matters arising on the high seas.

He must next decide whether to order a post mortem examination on the body and whether to hold an inquest. The outcome of the post mortem often decides this—the facts peculiar to every death dictate the course of action. For example, a doctor may refuse to certify the cause of death when called to a dead holiday-maker whom he has never seen before. Even if it seems the latter died from a heart attack, the doctor cannot be sure when he has not seen that person before, so he will certify death, but not the *cause* of death. The body is then reported to the coroner who will order a post mortem examination to establish the cause. A post mortem may reveal, for example, that death was due to a heart disease or a respiratory infection, or cancer. If death resulted from such purely natural causes, there will usually be no inquest. If however there has been an accident, an inquest will be necessary.

If a coroner is satisfied as to the cause of death, he will issue his 'pink form'—the burial order. He can issue this any time after viewing the body. The relatives take it to the registrar who will issue his certificate so that burial or cremation can proceed. Obviously, this only happens when deaths are reported to the coroner; normal deaths do not involve this type of action.

The Coroners (Amendment) Act 1926 gives power to a coroner to dispense with an inquest if the post mortem shows that death occurred from natural causes, but there are occasions when a coroner *must* by law hold an inquest. These include:

    (i) deaths from accidents, whether by road traffic or industry

H

(ii) deaths occurring in prison
(iii) violent deaths
(iv) unnatural deaths.

The word 'unnatural' has never been defined and is open to very wide interpretation. Arising from his medieval duty to value the chattels of deceased persons and felons, the coroner must hold an inquest on all executed persons. But the modern purpose is to identify the executed person and to determine whether judgement of death was duly carried out on the offender. A copy of this inquest must go to the sheriff and again this is a relic of the sheriff's duty to keep rolls on the coroners.

Apart from the statutory occasions when he must hold an inquest, a coroner will always hold one where there is any doubt over the cause of death, basing this on the word 'unnatural', and he relies almost entirely on the police for help in his investigations.

The Coroners (Amendment) Act 1926 says that a coroner *may* view the body, but in practice he always sees it when he decides to hold an inquest. It may happen that a body is destroyed or cannot be recovered. In these cases, a coroner must report the facts to the Home Secretary who may direct an inquest to be held, even though there is no body and therefore no post mortem.

An inquest of course, is not a medical examination. It is simply an enquiry, and a coroner must make sure that all information surrounding the death is at the inquest. The police obtain statements from witnesses and supply forms to the coroner. If possible, the paper work is done before the post mortem so the coroner has all the necessary information on hand. Some post mortems are held very soon after death, often before the police have had time to gather all the evidence for the inquest. In such cases the police would give an initial verbal account to the coroner and to the pathologist. The written work is completed in due course.

As already said, it is usually on the outcome of the post mortem that the coroner decides whether or not to hold an inquest. Other instances do arise, however. For example, when death is the result of, say, taking tablets or poison, the pathologist will defer his decision on the cause of death until organs from the body have been scientifically examined at a Forensic Science Laboratory. This may help to decide if the death was natural, accidental, self-inflicted or murder. Obviously this takes time and the result of the post mortem will be delayed. In such cases the coroner will open the inquest for purposes of identification only. The identity of the deceased must be proved to him beyond all doubt and he must be satisfied that the body is that of the person it purports to be. This is a formal part of every inquest and, once it is over, the funeral can proceed. The inquest can then be adjourned until the necessary evidence is available. This procedure is invariably adopted to prevent delay in the funeral arrangements and to help the mourning relatives.

AT THE INQUEST

Generally speaking, an inquest follows a fairly standard pattern. The coroner is in complete charge of the proceedings and his court is unlike a judicial court because there is no prosecution and no defence. An inquest is not a court which is designed to try a person; it is an enquiry as to the cause of death. Because of this, the rules of evidence in a criminal or civil court do not always apply. Leading questions, hearsay evidence and even evidence of opinion may be accepted by the coroner. If proceedings of a civil or criminal nature follow, then the evidence in such subsequent trials must conform to the standards laid down for those other courts. Coroners always try to follow the rules of evidence and a witness is not bound to answer questions which will incriminate him.

In many cases, a coroner will not sit alone at his inquest. He will have a jury of either men or women (or both) to assist him and, as pertains in a criminal court, the jury is representative of the general public. For a coroner's court, however, the only qualification for jurors is residence within the coroner's jurisdiction; their names do not have to be on the jurors' lists, nor even on the electoral registers. There is no property qualification either. It goes without saying that jurors must be competent, ie not lunatics or mental defectives, but there is no age limit for a coroner's jury. In practice, persons between twenty-one and sixty are chosen.

Membership of the jury may vary between 7 and 11, and each juror takes the following oath:

> I swear by Almighty God that I will diligently inquire and a true presentment make of all such matters and things as are here given me in charge on behalf of our Sovereign Lady the Queen, touching the death of . . . , now lying dead, and will, without fear or favour, affection or ill-will, a true verdict give according to the evidence.

A jury must be employed where, either before an inquest has begun, or in the course of one started without a jury, the coroner suspects:

    (i) the death occurred in prison, or in such a place or in such circumstances as to require an inquest under any Act of Parliament (apart from the Coroners Act 1887)

    (ii) the deceased came by his death through murder, manslaughter or infanticide

    (iii) that the death was caused by an accident, poisoning or disease, notice of which is required to a government department, or to any inspector or other officer of a government department, or in pursuance of any Act

    (iv) that the death was caused by an accident arising out of the use of a motor vehicle in a street or public place

    (v) that the death occurred in circumstances the continuance of, or possible recurrence of which, is prejudicial to the health or safety of the public, or any section of the public.

The coroner may also summon a jury in any other case where

he considers there is reason to do so, either before or during an inquest.

A juror who fails to appear at the appointed place and time, or who refuses to serve, may be fined up to £5. The coroner can summon witnesses to the inquest and they too may be fined for non-appearance. It is the coroner's duty to ensure that all witnesses, jurors, medical or scientific experts and other necessary persons are present. If he is dealing with an industrial accident, the appropriate government department must be told by him so that a representative can attend. On similar lines, when the accident involves motor vehicles and the driver of the offending car cannot be traced, the Home Secretary asks coroners to inform the Motor Insurers' Bureau. They may send a representative to the inquest to decide whether an *ex-gratia* payment can be made to the dependants of the deceased. The press and the public may attend, but if national security is involved the coroner may order that the inquest, or part of it, be held in private. Once he is satisfied that all necessary persons are present, he will open the proceedings.

The coroner will have before him a file which has been compiled by the police officer who investigated the incident—this man is the coroner's officer. The file will consist of statements by the witnesses and the coroner will question each in turn from the statements. As he examines each witness, who gives his evidence on oath, the coroner will write down what the witness says. This is in the form of another statement and, upon completion, it is signed by the witness who should read it first.

The first witness is usually someone to give the coroner the general background of the deceased. It may be a widow, a son, or any near relative and this person will give the deceased's age, state of health, occupation and other points which could have a bearing on his death. As an example, a coroner might ask questions on the deceased's health if this has some bearing on his driving, or questions about his eye-sight. This sort of information can best be given by close relatives.

Medical evidence is vitally important and the doctor who

attended the deceased may be called to give evidence. Doctors who attended him at death, or immediately after death, will be called and so will the pathologist who carried out the post mortem examination. He will be asked for his opinion and, if necessary, the scientists who examined portions of the body will also give evidence. In some cases, the coroner will accept a written certificate from such people if there is no dispute over their evidence. This is to obviate their unnecessary attendance.

Where there is a question of negligence—as might happen in a factory accident—the coroner will examine the person who ordered the deceased to perform the duty which led to his death, or who last maintained or checked the defective apparatus. It is not the function of a coroner's court to decide liability, but the family of the deceased can have their solicitor present to cross-examine each witness after the coroner has concluded his questioning.

The jury, if there is one, will of course be listening to the evidence and will receive any necessary guidance from the coroner. Its members will inspect any photographs or exhibits and, when the evidence has been heard, the coroner will formally state his findings. He will give the identity of the deceased, the date and place of his death and he will briefly repeat the evidence. If there is a jury, the decision as to cause of death is theirs although the coroner may assist with problems that arise. The jury will give the cause of death according to their joint decision—it might be 'murder by person or persons unknown', 'accidental death', 'suicide' or one of various other verdicts. Juries occasionally give strange verdicts. In 1931, a jury recorded that the deceased died possessed of an evil spirit!

If there is no jury, the coroner will state what he decides is the cause of death. It may be 'died from natural causes', 'misadventure' or some similar reason. An open verdict is recorded where the evidence has failed to establish a cause of death.

If a jury is in doubt, the coroner will direct them according to the evidence and it is at this stage that the coroner may find himself exercising an ancient power. The jury may arrive at a verdict of homicide; they may even go a stage further and name the person they feel is responsible. If no more than two jury members disagree, the verdict is valid and the coroner then has power to commit the suspect for trial at the next assizes. This power is very similar to that of the examining magistrates. The coroner can grant bail to the suspect even when the charge is one of murder, and he may bind over all witnesses to attend the assizes. He must notify this course of action to the Director of Public Prosecutions.

When a person is committed to the assizes by a coroner's court, the coroner will record this in a statement which has the effect of an indictment. If the suspect did not attend the inquest, the coroner can issue a warrant for his arrest and conveyance to the necessary assizes. If the suspect is at the inquest, he can be taken before an examining magistrate where the usual depositions will be taken.

Occasionally police investigations into a death may result in someone being arrested by them prior to the inquest. In this case, the justice's clerk would notify the coroner and the inquest would deal only with medical evidence as to the cause of death. It would then adjourn. The arrested person would be tried by the criminal court and, if convicted, the inquest would be closed. If, however, he was acquitted by the criminal court, the inquest would resume and might even consider his liability for some other crime not charged before the magistrates. A good example is where a person is acquitted by a criminal court of a charge of causing death by the dangerous driving of a motor cycle on a road. If this happens before the inquest is completed, the resumed inquest may produce a finding of manslaughter against that person. If this had been foreseen, the alternative charge would have been placed before the magistrates in the first instance, but even so it is possible to bring it. An accused may therefore find himself once more before the court on a different charge arising out of the same set of circumstances.

Liaison between the coroner and the police is strong and if the police inform the coroner that someone may be charged with murder, manslaughter or infanticide, or with causing death of the deceased by dangerous driving, the coroner must adjourn the inquest for fourteen days, or for any such further period as he thinks fit. This allows such problems to be sorted out and further adjournments are at the discretion of the coroner on application by the police. If criminal proceedings for any other offence arise out of the death, the practice is not to adjourn the inquest; instead the criminal charge is heard after conclusion of the inquest.

One facet of the coroner's inquest is the 'rider' which can be given by the jury. Riders include warnings about dangerous places such an unfenced quarries, deep canals and so on, and the rider will suggest improvements to make these places safe. They can also apply to an accident 'black-spot' and, because the press give riders a lot of publicity, a lot of good has resulted from them.

An inquest must not be confused with an official enquiry into a serious accident, such as a rail or air disaster, or a mining accident. In such cases there would be inquests upon the dead persons to establish their cause of death, but it would not seek the cause of the disaster. That would be the job of an official enquiry.

The Divisional Court can order an inquest to be held upon the application of the Attorney General, or it may order a fresh inquest if the findings are not consistent with the evidence before it. Similarly a new inquest can be ordered if fresh facts come to light. It is possible to quash an inquest if the aggrieved person applies to the right place and can be done by :

    (i) the High Court of Justice under its common law jurisdiction, whether the inquest contains a criminal charge or not. This is done by application for an order of certiorari

    (ii) the High Court under statutory powers upon application made by or under the authority of the Attorney General

    (iii) the court before whom any person criminally charged by the inquest is arraigned.

One of the most controversial aspects of the coroner's duties is his power to commit for trial a person accused by his inquest. This has long been subjected to argument and discussion by the judiciary, many of whom feel that this power should be removed. Between 1950 and 1966, 203 persons were committed for trial by coroners' juries; 15 were convicted of the offence charged, and 73 of a lesser offence. The power to commit for trial is not widely used. In 1966, a railway worker was committed by a coroner for trial on a charge of murder, but when the trial opened at the assizes, the police offered no evidence against the suspect and he was discharged.

Conversely, there are instances when an inquest has brought to justice a killer who would otherwise have escaped. One instance occurred in 1953 when a coroner was asked to adjourn an inquest upon the body of an illegitimate child which was found in a sack. He did this: the child's parents were charged before the magistrates with the offence of concealment of birth, and there followed repeated requests for adjournments until eventually the Director of Public Prosecutions said he was not proceeding with a charge of homicide. In the meantime, the couple married and, when the coroner resumed the inquest, his jury returned a verdict of murder against the man and infanticide against the mother. After medical evidence, the couple were sent to Leeds assizes on a coroner's indictment and were both found guilty of homicide (R v Conroy 1953).

The Council of the Law Society and the British Academy of Forensic Sciences think the office of coroner should be abolished but some other official would surely have to replace him. At the time of writing (1970), there is sitting the Brodrick Committee which was established in March 1965 by the Home Office to examine the law and practice relating to coroners, and to advise whether or not changes were desirable. To date, their recommendations have not been published and the coroner remains very much in charge of his unique and ancient court.

TREASURE TROVE

There is a wealth of romance surrounding the finding of buried treasure and thousands of pounds worth is dug up every year in England alone. Much of it is found on building sites or during the construction of new roads, although ordinary people such as householders and farmers constantly discover hidden treasure. Some of it will undoubtedly be classified as treasure trove, whilst a lot will find its way into museums or into the hands of the finder or landowner without it being so classified.

So what is the definition of treasure trove? Namely, that it consists of gold or silver in coin, plate or bullion which has been *hidden* in any house or in the earth or other secret place, the owner thereof being unknown. It belongs to the sovereign, or to some other lord or other person by the sovereign's grant or prescription. If the person who hid it can be found, it belongs to him. The definition rules out hidden jewels, glassware, pottery or metal, other than gold or silver. In fact it rules out everything which is not gold or silver, unless such objects are set in gold or silver. If there is any doubt as to whether a discovery is treasure trove, the coroner of the district must be informed.

It has been shown in the preceding pages, that the modern coroner is chiefly concerned with sudden deaths; but it will be remembered that his origin dates from the time when he was keeper of the king's pleas. He was then a clerk dealing with the collection of chance revenues. Treasure trove is such a revenue. Those early coroners were in effect tax-gatherers and in order to avoid tax, payment of which has been disliked from earliest times, many people would hide their valuables. They hid coins up chimneys, or dug a hole in the ground; they used hollow trees and other curious places to keep their hard-earned wealth for themselves. When a hoard of such coins, or silver or gold plate, is found, then the Crown wants its fair share, long-overdue though it is. It is still the coroner's duty to see that is done.

This duty has remained with him throughout the ages while

other chance revenues have been overtaken with the passage of time, or taken over by other officials. Wrecks, for example, are now dealt with by the Receiver of Wrecks, whilst the deodand and the forfeited chattels of felons have disappeared. One duty that still remains concerns the royal fish—the sturgeon. Any sturgeon is still legally the property of the Crown, as it has been since Edward II ruled that all such fish caught in English waters so belonged. It was the coroner's job to see that this ruling was carried out and today the provision still appears to exist, although there is no penalty for disobedience of this law. This ancient privilege is to be abolished.

To revert to treasure trove, the coroner's job is to decide by holding an inquest, whether or not gold or silver was deliberately *hidden*. This can often be decided by the manner in which it was stored—up a chimney, or encased in an urn beneath the ground. Gold found in a field, or in a river, may not be treasure trove because it was probably lost and not hidden. Lost coins can never be treasure trove because they are not hidden. His duties here were laid down by *De Officio Coronatis* in 1276—he must enquire of treasure that is found, who were the finders and who is suspected thereof.

If a coroner decides that a particular treasure is trove, it must go to the Crown, although the finder will be paid the market value for it, perhaps by the British Museum. Had the finder kept it and not informed the coroner, it would have been taken from him when eventually his discovery came to light. In that event, he would gain no benefit from it, and would, until 1 January 1969, technically have been guilty of a common law misdemeanour and liable to punishment by fine or imprisonment. The offence of concealment of treasure trove was abolished by the Theft Act 1968; theft of such property might now be considered instead.

Quite often a coroner will decide that treasure is not treasure trove, in which case he does not decide ownership and it belongs to the landowner, or possibly to the person who found it. In cases of dispute, a civil court action would determine the true ownership because high values are sometimes involved.

Each year brings more reports of valuables being found. In 1966, coins worth £30,000 were unearthed in Nottinghamshire. In 1968, a gold cross was found in a Kentish field; it brought £5,000 for the finder. In 1969 there were two finds, one of gold coins and one of silver coins, the total value of which was in excess of £50,000. In May 1970 a Celtic necklace, over 2,000 years old, was declared treasure trove after being used as a plaything by children. It was so valuable that no estimate was put on it.

Even today people are hiding cash in their homes; if by any remote chance it consists of gold or silver it might well be declared treasure trove in the future if the owner forgets about it, or dies without saying where it is. This means the nation will get it, and its value will go to the finder. This makes hoarding rather senseless.

SIX

Appeals, Legal Aid And Bail

APPEALS

The Criminal Appeal Act 1966 divided the Court of Appeal into two distinct parts. On the one hand there is the Civil Division dealing with appeals from the High Court and from county courts, and on the other is the Criminal Division. This hears appeals from assizes, quarter sessions and the High Court.

Before this, the Court of Appeal coped with civil cases while the Court of Criminal Appeal catered for the criminals. The former came into existence with the passing of the Judicature Act 1873 and the latter was founded in 1907. These were housed in the Royal Courts of Justice in the Strand, London, and this is still the home of the appeal courts under their new names. The highest appeal court in the land is still the House of Lords.

There has apparently been a right of appeal against judicial decisions from the earliest times. During the Roman occupation for example, there was right of final appeal to the emperor, and in Anglo-Saxon times appeals were heard by the local county courts of those days. Appeals were also heard by the witanagemot and finally by the king in council. Around 1066 there were two supreme courts. One, the Exchequer Court, was made a court of appeal by Edward III in 1357; the other was known as the Supreme Court of Justice for Greater Causes. Another court of appeal was instituted by Elizabeth I in 1585 to hear appeals from the Court of Queen's Bench.

In the middle ages appeal by battle was popular. This was known as trial by battle or even the assize of battle and extended to everyone and every type of case, particularly murder and treason. It was supposedly introduced to this country from Normandy. This method of appeal was accepted by the Court of Common Pleas, but in 1571 Elizabeth tried to stop it. Nonetheless, it continued well into the nineteenth century! On 8 August 1817, Abraham Thornton was acquitted at Warwick Assizes of the murder of Mary Ashford. Her brother, William, disagreed with the court and appealed to King's Bench Division against the decision. Thornton appeared on 17 November in that year, but in court he threw down his glove and challenged his accuser to mortal combat. He claimed he had a legal right to do this. The court examined his claim and on 16 April 1818 they decided that Thornton could legally claim appeal by combat, however obsolete it seemed. The girl's brother, however, refused to fight on the grounds that he was too young. The prisoner was therefore discharged. His unusual appeal had succeeded but it resulted, in 1819, of the repeal of that ancient law.

Today, not directly as a result of that case, appeals are more civilised. They come in various forms and for various reasons, civil and criminal.

Mention ought to be made of the ecclesiastical appeals, for they helped to frame our judicial system. There was right of appeal through the archbishop to the provincial synod from decisions of the bishops in their own court. There may have been appeal to a general council, but there was also right of appeal to the Vatican in Rome. Saint Wilfred had tried to introduce a system of final appeal to Rome somewhere around AD 694, but did not succeed. It was in 1151, almost five hundred years later, that a final appeal to the Vatican was introduced. This resulted from the work of the papal legate, Henry de Blois, bishop of Winchester, but there were drawbacks such as the distance and time involved in travelling to Rome.

Not many years later, in 1164, Henry II said that all appeals in ecclesiastical matters should be from the archdeacon to the diocesan, from the diocesan to the archbishop, and from the archbishop to the king. Appeals could not go beyond the king without royal assent, but in spite of this several did reach the pope. Under Henry VIII's Reformation, however, the system disappeared altogether in 1553; he made it an offence to appeal to Rome and anyone who disobeyed was guilty of *praemuniere* which was in effect the introduction of a foreign power into the land. In this case, the foreign power was the pope.

There was a High Court of Delegates which heard appeals from the ecclesiastical courts and from Admiralty. This disappeared in 1833 when the Privy Council took over.

Apart from the ecclesiastical appeals, which played such an important part in the formation of the English legal system, there was right of appeal in civil and criminal cases, even before courts were established specifically for that purpose. There has always been right of appeal to the sovereign and this was often based on the king's mood of the moment rather than upon legal provisions. Nonetheless, it did exist and the law first recognised appeals in the Statute of Westminster II in 1285. This allowed for the correction of errors by the judges of King's Bench, or in the Court of Common Pleas whether in civil or criminal matters, and the smaller courts were included too. If a claim arose it would be considered by a judge although there was no court to deal specifically with complaints of errors.

The early common law appeals were by writs of tolt and pone and false judgements. A writ of tolt was used to remove a case concerning title of land from a manor court to a county court. It was based either on a delay or a denial of justice and often happened when a steward of a manor failed to give a decision. A writ of pone took a case from the ancient county court to a court of common pleas. This was used when a sheriff failed to administer justice. A writ of false judgement was used when a manor court or a county court delivered an erroneous verdict. If land was involved, it was heard by the Court of Common Pleas, but all other cases went to King's Bench. The Provisions of Westminster 1259 said that writs of false judgement must be decided only in the royal courts. A false judgement was based on some procedural irregularity and to satisfy an appellant the case could be sent back to the local court from the royal court, or else a new trial could be ordered in a royal court.

Errors of law, as a ground of appeal, were rare because the law was in its infancy at this time. A writ of error was used to quash the judgements of courts of record, which included the common pleas court, assizes, general eyre, borough chartered courts and various local courts. They were known as courts of record because they had to keep a record of their proceedings, and this did not apply to some manor courts or the early county courts.

King's Bench, however, established a right to hear appeals brought by a writ of error from the Court of Common Pleas. It next tried to win superiority over the Exchequer Court on similar grounds but the barones opposed these claims and in 1358, the first Court of Exchequer Chamber was established. It consisted of the Lord Chancellor and the Lord Treasurer who met, later with judges, in the form of a discussion at either the Great Chamber of the Exchequer at Westminster or at one of the Serjeant's Inns. Their duty was to settle doubts raised in other courts and this court also served as a tribunal of appeal from the courts of Exchequer. It seems this discussion group stems from the habit of chancellors seeking judicial advice from the judges on points of law. Any chief justice or chief barone could refer points of law to this court for a decision and all available judges debated the issue. A majority decision was accepted and this established a precedent.

In 1585 Elizabeth I extended this court to include erroneous judgements in Queen's Bench and further Acts of Parliament extended and ratified its powers and jurisdiction. There were some problems with this court; for one thing it was never possible to guarantee the attendance of the Lord Chancellor and the Lord Treasurer. Because of this, the chief justices of Queen's Bench and Common Pleas were empowered in 1589 to act as delegates. Their decisions and rulings could always be countermanded by the Lords Chancellor and Treasurer. There was always further appeal from this court to the House of Lords; it became an extremely busy court, but ended in 1830.

So far as discussions at Sergeant's Inn were concerned, they discontinued in respect of civil cases in the reign of Charles II, but the system remained for criminal cases. In 1848, however, the Court for Crown Cases Reserved was established to cope with such appeals. It consisted of five judges from the common law courts with the Lord Chief Justice as president. A defendant had no right of appeal to this court—cases were sent there by the assize court judges or chairmen of quarter sessions at their discretion and the issues involved points of law, evidential and procedural matters. In practice, a case was sent to this court after the verdict had been given, but before sentence had been pronounced. The judge (or the chairman) reserved his final decision on the punishment until the Court for Crown Cases Reserved had reached its conclusion.

The Judicature Act 1873 did not abolish this court although in 1907 it was superseded by the Court of Criminal Appeal. There was formerly also a court of Appeal in Chancery but, under the Judicature Act, this was amalgamated with the Court of Appeal.

Criminal appeals

The Court of Criminal Appeal consisted of the Lord Chief Justice and judges of Queen's Bench Division in an uneven number; three constituted a quorum. In practice it consisted of the Lord Chief Justice and two others. This court dealt with appeals from quarter sessions, assizes, the Central Criminal Court and the Crown courts. There was no right of appeal against acquittal, but after conviction there could be an appeal on the following points:

(i) On any point of law
(ii) With leave of the trial judge or the Court of Criminal Appeal, on fact or law or both, or any other sufficient ground
(iii) With leave of the Court of Criminal Appeal against sentence (unless the sentence was one fixed by law).

The court had very wide powers and could dismiss an appeal, quash a conviction, alter or vary a sentence, or even substitute a conviction for another offence if it appeared that the accused ought, on the evidence, to have been convicted of that, rather

I

than the one for which he was convicted.

Under the Criminal Appeal Act 1964 the court could order a new trial when fresh evidence came to light. The functions of this court have been taken over by the new Court of Appeal (Criminal Division) and all legislation governing criminal appeals was consolidated in the Criminal Appeal Act 1968.

The Court of Appeal (Criminal Division). This court, founded in 1966, consists of the Lord Chief Justice, the Master of the Rolls and judges from the Court of Appeal. When in session, there must be at least three judges. The Lord Chief Justice may, after consulting the Master of the Rolls, request any of the judges of Queen's Bench Division to sit as a member of this court. A judge, however, cannot sit in a court of appeal on a case in which he acted as judge in the first instance.

Although the court usually sits with three judges, this number is increased to five or seven or even more (always an odd number) when a point is of exceptional public importance. A majority decision is accepted. The court always sits in London, but more than one court may sit at any one time.

The court has the power to hear fresh evidence and can order a new trial after it; it can also order a new trial when an old one was null and void through some irregularity. It has power to quash a conviction or a sentence, and even to substitute a verdict of guilty for an offence not charged, but found proven by the evidence now before the court. These powers were held by the now defunct Court of Criminal Appeal.

Under the 1968 Act, a person who wishes to appeal must give notice of appeal, or must apply for leave to appeal, within twenty-eight days of his conviction or sentence. The court can extend this period and, if the appellant is poor, a counsel and sometimes a solicitor may be assigned to him. His application for leave to appeal must be in writing. Strangely enough, he has no right to be present when his application is heard although he can attend his appeal proper, unless it is a matter of pure law. A transcript of the case and notes by the judge who first tried the appellant must be given to the appeal court. An appeal may be on fact or law. A person convicted on indictment may appeal to the Court of Appeal (Criminal Division) on the following grounds:

(i) Against conviction which involves only a question of law

(ii) With leave of the Court of Appeal (Criminal Division) or of the judge who first tried the case, he may appeal against conviction on a question of fact, or mixed fact and law, or any other ground which the court regards as sufficient to warrant an appeal

(iii) With leave of the Court of Appeal (Criminal Division), he may appeal against sentence passed on his conviction unless the sentence is fixed by law.

A person who has been committed by the magistrates' court to either quarter sessions or assizes for sentence has right of appeal to this court against sentence. He can appeal if:

(i) He was sentenced to six months imprisonment or more, either for that offence or that offence with other offences dealt with at the same time

(ii) The sentence is one the court had no power to impose

(iii) He is the subject of a deportation order, or is disqualified from driving, or if an order is made which lifts the suspension of a sentence.

There is also a right of appeal from a coroner's court to the Court of Appeal (Criminal Division) against verdicts of not guilty by reason of insanity, or a finding of unfitness to plead.

There is a further right of appeal from the Court of Appeal (Criminal Division) to the House of Lords. This only applies where the Court of Appeal (Criminal Division) has certified that the matter involves a point of law of general public importance. In addition to this certificate, however, there must be leave to appeal from either the Court of Appeal (Criminal Division) or the Lords themselves. Either the prosecution or the defence can appeal to the Lords.

In spite of the apparent finality of appeals to the House of

Lords, execution of sentence can be further postponed or even remitted. A postponement, often called a reprieve, is granted by the queen or by a judge. If the defendant becomes insane after judgement, such reprieve must be granted by a court. Remission of execution of judgement, known as a pardon, is granted only at the discretion of the Crown. Pardons can be conditional or absolute, on recommendation by the Home Secretary. They can relate to part of an offence, which means the sentence is commuted to a lesser punishment.

Civil appeals

Civil appeals are necessarily varied and can be dealt with only briefly in these pages. The following is therefore a general outline.

The Judicature Act of 1925 gives right of appeal to the Civil Division of the Court of Appeal from a judgement or order of the High Court. This appeal court has jurisdiction to hear motions for a new trial after a trial by jury. There is also right of appeal from a Queen's Bench Master to a judge in chambers and then possibly to the Court of Appeal (Civil Division). On certain issues an appeal can be made direct to the Court of Appeal from a decision of the Masters. Appeals from district registrars lie in circumstances similar to those from Queen's Bench Masters. An appeal will lie from an official referee to the Court of Appeal (Civil Division) on a point of law and from a decision on a question of fact relevant to a charge of fraud or breach of professional duty. An appeal from a judge in chambers now goes to the Court of Appeal (Civil Division) and not to a divisional court as was formerly the case.

There are cases when there can be no appeal to the Court of Appeal (Civil Division). These are known as 'appeal barred' and are as follows:

(i) From an order which has extended the time for appealing
(ii) From a judge's order granting unconditional leave to defend an action

(iii) From a decision of a judge declared by statute to be final
(iv) Where the parties have agreed to exclude the right of appeal and the agreement has been embodied in the order
(v) Where the party is estopped by his conduct since judgement
(vi) Where the appellant has been stated to be a 'vexatious litigant' and has been refused leave to sue.

In some instances leave to appeal must be first obtained from either the Court of Appeal itself, or from a lower court, but this is not a general rule. It is possible in some cases to appeal to the Court of Appeal (Civil Division) without leave. Leave is required where the appeal is :

(i) From the determination by a divisional court of any appeal to that court
(ii) From an order of the High Court which was made with the consent of the parties and was as to costs only which by law are left to the court's discretion
(iii) From an interlocutory order or judgement made or given by a judge.

No leave to appeal is necessary where the liberty of a subject or the custody of a child is concerned, or where an injunction or the appointment of a receiver is granted or refused. In all other cases there is right of appeal to the Court of Appeal (Civil Division).

An appeal commences by the issue of a notice which must state whether all or part of a judgement is to be subject of the appeal, and the grounds must be specified. The same procedure applies whether the application is by way of appeal or for a new trial. Notice of appeal must generally be served within six months from the judgement or order.

The Court of Appeal (Civil Division) will re-hear a case and under some circumstances will admit new evidence. When it comes to the decision, the court has all the powers of the High Court and may, on hearing an appeal :

(i) Order a new trial
(ii) Set aside the verdict or judgement
(iii) Substitute a proper sum where the jury has awarded damages which are either excessive or inadequate. The parties must consent to this action, otherwise the case will be sent back for re-assessment by another jury. (*Note*: Very few civil cases come before a jury; the Court of Appeal is often called upon to consider amounts awarded by judges sitting alone).

There is no appeal from a county court, without leave of the judge, if the claim does not exceed £20. If a claim exceeds £200, there may be a claim on facts in most cases, and the judge of the county court might be asked for a note of the findings of law and fact.

A new trial may be ordered by the Court of Appeal (Civil Division) where a county court judge wrongly admitted or rejected evidence. This is an appeal against a legal ruling, as admissibility of evidence is a matter of law, not fact. No new trial of findings of fact may be ordered. If a county court judge does not order a fresh trial, the Court of Appeal (Civil Division) will order retrial under a different judge.

Appeal can be made from the Court of Appeal (Civil Division) to the House of Lords, but leave of this court, or leave of the Lords, must be given. If not, the appeal must be certified as reasonable by two counsel and must be lodged within three months. It will be heard by at least three judges who are Lords of Appeal, and they may be the Lord Chancellor, the Lords of Appeal in Ordinary or such peers who hold or have held high judicial office.

Appeals in the lower criminal courts. A person convicted by a magistrates' court may appeal to quarter sessions:

(i) Against sentence, if he pleaded guilty
(ii) Against conviction and/or sentence if he pleaded not guilty
(iii) Against sentence if sentenced for an offence in respect

of which he was previously put on probation or conditionally discharged.

The word 'sentence' does not include:

(i) A probation order or an order for a conditional discharge
(ii) An order to pay costs
(iii) An order for the destruction of an animal (ie dangerous dog)
(iv) An order made under any enactment which allows the court no discretion.

The appellant must give to the clerk of the court and the other parties, fourteen days written notice of his appeal. This time limit can be extended by quarter sessions. The appeal can be abandoned if the appellant gives written notice of his intentions to the clerk and to the court not later than three days before the hearing. He might, however, be ordered to pay costs.

When an appellant is in custody, he can generally be released on bail to appear at the appeal court, unless the case involves committal to quarter sessions for sentence for borstal training, or for conviction for an indictable offence.

There is no right of appeal to quarter sessions against dismissal of a case, except in bastardy and excise cases, although there is right of application for a case stated (see below).

The decision of quarter sessions on an appeal against a conviction or sentence is final when questions of fact are involved. But if a point of law is involved, the outcome might be a case stated for the opinion of Queen's Bench Division.

A person convicted on a coroner's indictment or at a quarter sessions as an incorrigible rogue under the Vagrancy Act 1824, may appeal to the Criminal Division of the Court of Appeal on a question of law, or with leave on a question of fact, or mixed fact and law, or with leave, against sentence.

A defendant or a prosecutor may appeal to the House of Lords from a decision of a divisional court of Queen's Bench Division in a criminal case or matter, or from any decision of the Criminal Division of the Court of Appeal after appeal to that court.

Appeal by Case Stated. The Magistrates' Courts Act 1952 allows a person to appeal by way of case stated. This method is open to anyone who was a party to any proceedings before a magistrates' court. It includes persons aggrieved by the conviction, order, determination or other proceedings of the court and they may question the proceedings on the grounds that they were either wrong in law, or in excess of jurisdiction. This is done by requesting the justices who sat in the court in question to 'state a case' in the court for the opinion of the High Court.

There must be a question of law or jurisdiction and such applications must be made within fourteen days of the court's original decision. They cannot be made in respect of decisions which themselves carry a right of appeal to the High Court.

The magistrates may decline to state a case if they feel the application is too frivolous, but they must give the applicant a certificate to that effect. The applicant on the other hand can apply to the High Court for a writ of mandamus to order the magistrates to state a case. Applications for writs of mandamus are heard by the Divisional Court. Either side may ask for a case stated on a point of law. Furthermore, quarter sessions, on hearing an appeal from a magistrates' court, may also be asked to state a case for the opinion of Queen's Bench Division.

The effect of a case stated is really akin to an appeal on a point of law. There is no power to state a case when a defendant has elected for trial by jury. A case stated is not limited to the points of law which were argued in the magistrates' court and the other parties concerned should agree on a draft statement of the facts which govern their particular problem. The magistrates must state a case within three months and, if they fail in this, the writ of mandamus can compel them to do so.

When the case stated reaches the divisional court, several avenues are open. If that court decides that the defendant has not committed the offence charged, they will return the case to the magistrates with an order to acquit the defendant. This acquittal is final—there is no appeal against it. On the other hand if the divisional court feels that, in law, an offence has been committed by the accused, it will return the case and direct a conviction. It may be that the divisional court decides that the facts relate to an offence which was not charged. In these cases they can amend the conviction and substitute the correct offence. This seldom occurs because a defendant may produce evidence which is sufficient to secure his acquittal on one of these secondary charges.

Appeal by way of case stated is not allowed where a statute gives the magistrates the final decision over an offence, because this is lasting and binding. There is no appeal and no case stated from it.

Occasionally a magistrates' court may act without jurisdiction and in these cases the Queen's Bench Division may be asked for an order of certiorari to quash the conviction, or an order of prohibition to prevent them exceeding their jurisdiction. An order of certiorari may also be granted if a trial is unfair, or if some member of a bench has a personal interest in the case. In such events, application for certiorari must be made within six months after leave to apply is first granted.

The magistrates may be represented and compile affidavits giving the reasons for their decisions. When a conviction is quashed, the convicted person must be released and his punishment revoked. He will not stand trial again for that offence.

Stated cases are not common because few summary trials involve contested points of law. But when eventually the Court of Queen's Bench makes its decision, it carries authoritative precedence. The law stated in these cases becomes a binding authority on all lower courts.

Examining justices cannot state a case because their court is not a court of summary jurisdiction. Cases can be stated only in courts of summary jurisdiction, although it can be done by the licensing justices.

An example of points of law involving a case stated might be given in, say, a prosecution for furiously riding or driving a carriage. It has been held that a bicycle is a carriage for these purposes but, if the aggrieved person felt his bicycle was not a 'carriage', he could ask the magistrates to state a case on this point. The divisional court would then have to decide whether a bicycle was a carriage. If they said not, the defendant would win his point, and because the wording of the statute says 'furiously riding a carriage' and not a bicycle, then his case would be dismissed and he would not be guilty of any offence.

As a matter of interest, Taylor v Goodwin (1879) decided that a bicycle is a carriage and, as a result, anyone who rides one to the danger or annoyance of persons may be guilty of an offence of 'furiously driving or riding a carriage'—this is the wording of the Act which creates the offence. In the case of Ellis v Nott-Bower (1896) it was held that a bicycle was a vehicle. These cases have established for all time that a bicycle is a vehicle and that it is also a carriage. Any statutes which use these words now include bicycles in the offences they create. This is the sort of problem solved by stating a case for the opinion of the High Court.

LEGAL AID

Since the fifteenth century, there has been a system of legal aid in Scotland for both civil and criminal proceedings. So far as England is concerned, Magna Carta said that none should be denied the right of justice, but because legal fees have always been high, the poor man was often unable to take his problems to court.

In England there is little reference to legal aid until the nineteenth century. In a case of 1875, a form of aid was provided in civil cases by an ancient procedure known as in forma pauperis, but even so the facility was virtually unknown. At the turn of the century, there was a slight development: the Criminal Appeal Act of 1907 made some provision for aid and this was helped by both the Poor Prisoners Defence Act of 1930 and the Summary Jurisdiction (Appeals) Act of 1933.

By 1939, the notion of free legal assistance was gaining ground in both civil and criminal proceedings but much of it depended upon charitable organisations or upon newspapers. The most important step came as recently as 1949 when the Legal Aid and Advice Act of that year became law.

Legal aid in civil cases

Even though the *in forma pauperis* procedure had been in force from as early as the fifteenth century, it was seldom used. For one thing, ever since 1494, a person holding more than £5 of capital could not take part in the scheme. £5 may have been a moderate sum in the fifteenth century, but by the time the poorer people had use for the courts, as litigants, the value of that £5 had shrunk so the *in forma pauperis* procedure was of little practical value.

It was not until 1883 that the figure was increased to the more realistic sum of £25. Even so, it was barely used. In 1895, no reports of its use occurred before Queen's Bench Division or the Court of Appeal and for some reason it was thought not to apply to county courts, even though they had been created to cater especially for the poor. There was nothing to bar it from these courts.

Over the turn of the century, some charities became interested in the plight of poor persons faced with legal proceedings. From this, it was suggested that there be compiled a rota of solicitors and barristers who were willing to act without a fee, but the idea did not reach fruition. In 1906, however, there were demands for better facilities to fight legal contests and at this time there was a popular but unconventional system which involved the payment of small weekly amounts for future use in legal actions. Unfortunately this was misused by dishonest practitioners. Nonetheless, things were moving, and in 1909 the Gorell Committee on County Courts, together with the Royal Commission on Divorce, paid close attention to the lack of legal aid.

In 1910 new rules for the *in forma pauperis* procedure were drafted. One of these hoped to increase the capital allowance to £50 and the long promised list of solicitors and counsel willing to act for poor persons was drawn up. But as before, this scheme was never put into operation. The draft rules were revived in 1913 but were again postponed. Finally in 1914 they were put into operation but were promptly hampered by World War I.

Nonetheless, the efforts to create an acceptable type of legal aid continued. Committees sat in the twenties and eventually, in 1926, the Rules of the Supreme Court (Poor Persons) Order 1925 came into force. This never produced the desired result and very little happened until the Legal Aid and Advice Act 1949. Thus, so far as the civil cases were concerned, the effective date was 2 October 1950, but some sections of the Act did not come into force until as late as 1960. These sections brought civil cases in the House of Lords, quarter sessions and magistrates' courts within the scope of this legislation.

Today legal aid is designed to help persons of small means to bring or defend court actions free of cost. It is not available in cases of defamation, breach of promise, seduction or enticement. Before legal aid is granted, the applicant must show:

(i) He is financially incapable of paying the costs
(ii) The case in question can be justified.

There is also a means test. Assistance will be given, with or without contribution, if the applicant's disposable income is less than £700 per annum, and whose disposable capital is less than £500. These provisions are contained in the Legal Aid Act 1960 and the means test rests with the Department of Health & Social Security whose decision is final.

A person's income is based on his wages for the last twelve months, less expenses connected with his employment. The annual income tax payable is also deducted, together with rent and any maintenance which is payable. If the applicant owns a house, its capital value is calculated as one-half of the amount by which, after deduction for mortgages, it exceeds £2,000. Capital repayments together with an allowance for repairs and rates are also deducted.

When an applicant has capital over £500, he must prove that he cannot proceed unless he is aided, but even so he is liable to contribute towards his costs if they amount to over £125.

Legal aid is not allowed when an applicant's costs are covered by insurance, nor if he belongs to any association, such as a trade union, which is willing to assist. Special provisions exist for trustees and executors who are not, in themselves, entitled to legal aid.

The applicant must convince a local legal aid committee that he has a *prima facie* case or defence. If the committee refuses a legal aid certificate, it must give its reasons and there is appeal to the area committee, whose decision is final. The scheme is administered by the legal profession and panels of barristers and solicitors willing to co-operate are drawn up. From these, the litigants select their solicitors or counsel provided, of course, the litigant is in possession of a legal aid certificate. A copy of this must be supplied to the counsel.

Legal aid in criminal cases

The struggle for legal aid in criminal cases followed the same lines as that for civil cases. Prior to the turn of the century, much aid came from charitable organisations or from newspapers who helped an accused person. The case of Adolph Beck, a Norwegian businessman who suffered a miscarriage of justice at the hands of the English criminal courts, was largely responsible for the creation of the Court of Criminal Appeal. When the Court was established in 1907, there were rules which governed appeals and which further said that no prisoner would be without legal aid. Even so, there was no aid for persons on summary trial. A high proportion of criminal cases were heard and dealt with by this method, ie at magistrates' courts, and in 1924 the Magistrates Association expressed deep concern at the situation and quoted occasions where poor people were imprisoned because their defence had not been shown to the court. After a great deal of discussion by committees, the Law Society and the government, the Poor Prisoners Defence Act of 1930 became law. It provided that anyone charged with an indictable offence, who had insufficient means to pay for his defence, could be granted a defence certificate if it was considered necessary in the interests of justice. In cases of murder, the granting of a defence certificate was obligatory. A legal aid certificate could also be granted by the magistrates for summary trials, and for preliminary hearings, ie committal proceedings.

Legal aid for appeals was covered by the Summary Jurisdiction (Appeals) Act 1933 but, as with civil cases, the real breakthrough did not arrive until the 1949 Act which established a legal aid fund. Today when examining magistrates are considering whether to commit someone for trial, they may request that a solicitor, or if necessary counsel, be assigned to defend the prisoner. Their expenses, and assistance for persons legally aided, are paid out of the fund which runs at a loss. Contributions by litigants, costs and damages are paid in. A single magistrate may grant legal aid, and so can a judge of assize or the chairman of quarter sessions. Nonetheless, a legal aid certificate can be granted only if certain conditions are fulfilled. These are: the prisoner must be too poor to pay for his own defence; the interests of justice demand that such a certificate be granted.

From 1 October 1968, the coming into force of sections 73 and 75 of the Criminal Justice Act 1967 has governed the power of magistrates to grant legal aid in criminal cases. This Act also introduced a contribution scheme for legal aid. It can now be granted by the magistrates:

    (i) For proceedings before a magistrates' court
    (ii) For an appeal to quarter sessions
    (iii) For the expenses of the trial, when a person is committed for trial to assizes or quarter sessions.

Likewise, a court of assize or quarter sessions can order that a person be given legal aid for proceedings before these courts. The Court of Appeal (Criminal Division) can similarly order legal aid for those who appeal against sentence or conviction and this can be given either on the application for leave to appeal, or on the actual appeal itself. This latter court can also order legal aid for a person appealing to the House of Lords.

There are two occasions when legal aid *must* be granted. They are:

   (i) When a person is committed for trial for murder

  (ii) When the prosecution appeals or applies for leave to appeal to the House of Lords from the Court of Appeal.

In all other cases, the granting of legal aid is discretionary. It is always based on the fact that a person whose means are insufficient to meet costs should be aided, and that it is necessary in the interests of justice.

Before a court makes a legal aid order, the applicant must furnish a written statement of his means on a prescribed form and he may be required to make an immediate payment on account of any contribution towards legal aid costs. The question of how much will be decided, and any necessary adjustments will be made at the hearing. The courts are empowered to make a contribution order towards the legal aid costs as appears reasonable having regard to the means of the applicant. If the applicant is under eighteen, the court will consider the means of his parent or guardian.

Application for legal aid can be made orally at a court, or to the justices' clerk on the prescribed application form. Applications made before a magistrates' court can be made by arrested persons and also by those summoned or bailed to appear; even a person who has not yet appeared can apply, but his application must be dealt with by the court before which he is due to appear.

A person in custody may not always know which court he will attend and the police will take steps to notify him as soon as possible so that he can make the necessary application. Notices giving the up-to-date position regarding legal aid in criminal cases are on display at all police stations.

BAIL

The word comes from the Norman French meaning safekeeping and is today defined as a recognisance or bond taken by a duly authorised person to ensure the appearance of an accused at an appointed place and time to answer the charge made against him.

The granting of bail is based on the presumption that an accused person is innocent until proved guilty and that he should not be unnecessarily kept in custody. Whenever possible, an untried person is released on bail, but due regard is given to the nature of the charge, the safety of the accused and of witnesses, and other relevant factors. In the seventeenth century, bail was regarded as important because no provision was made for feeding the prisoners and many died through starvation!

Like many legal practices which are today regarded as standard, the origins of bail are obscure, having been lost through the passage of time. It may have started in Saxon times.

The Statute of Westminster I in 1275 listed the persons described as bailable, plus a few who were not. The effects of this statute were reinforced by later laws. By 1484, under Richard III, a justice of the peace could grant bail, but some persons abused this facility with the result that, in 1487, it was laid down that two justices were required.

Bail is found in numerous early statutes and most of them guarded against excessive bail. Exactly what 'excessive' means has always been left to a court's discretion. In its undefined meaning, excessive bail was banned by the Bill of Rights of 1689 which still prevails, but there have been some high bail figures. As long ago as 1925, three London bankers accused of fraudulent conversion were each granted bail of £10,000; but as a rough guide, bail is regarded as excessive if it exceeds the maximum fine for the offence charged.

Today the granting of bail is widely practised and members of the public often think that a person released on bail actually hands over a sum of money to the officials. This is not so in England. The object is to set at liberty a person who is arrested or imprisoned, on condition that some security is given in return. The security is to ensure that he will appear at a given place and time to answer any charges, but it does not mean that cash is handed over. If the accused disappears, or does not answer his bail, a sum is then forfeited. It is in effect a contract; when a person is released on bail in, say, a sum of £25, he will forfeit that sum if he does not turn up at the given time and place. He has broken the contract. If someone stood as a surety for him, then unfortunately that person will lose his money.

Procedure for granting bail

Bail may be granted by :

    (i) A police officer of or above the rank of inspector, or the officer in charge of a police station, irrespective of rank

    (ii) The judiciary (ranging from any judge down to magistrates)

    (iii) A coroner

    (iv) The governor of a prison, but only by the direction of a justice, or a judge in chambers.

Bail can be granted to a person charged with any offence, even murder and treason, but in practice is seldom granted to persons charged with very serious offences. Where murder is concerned, it is possible that the charge, as shown by the evidence available, might be one of justifiable homicide when bail would not be unusual. For treason, however, bail can only be granted by the order of a High Court judge or the Secretary of State.

When the question of bail is considered by a magistrates' court, or at quarter sessions or by a coroner, and they refuse it, the accused person may appeal to the High Court. He may also do this if the terms of bail are not acceptable to him. In these cases the High Court may admit him to bail or may direct that this be done, or they may vary the conditions or reduce the amount of surety involved.

Other considerations must be borne in mind when bail is requested and these include the nature of the charge, and whether or not it is practicable to bring the prisoner before a

K

court within twenty-four hours. Generally speaking, if a person cannot be brought before such a court, and if the offence is not a serious one, he will be released on bail. Other points to be borne in mind include:

(i) The likelihood of the prisoner appearing at court
(ii) His age
(iii) Whether there is a sufficiency of sureties
(iv) Whether he is arrested on warrant or otherwise
(v) What evidence there is to support the charge.

With regard to these, the general demeanour and history of a prisoner will help decide the issues raised in (i) above—a prisoner with no fixed address is clearly a risk. The age is important (see iv below). The prisoner might be attacked; he might be compelled by fear not to appear, or he might be extremely violent; all this must be considered. Furthermore, thought must be given to the possibility of intimidation of witnesses, the previous character of the accused, and other salient points. The proper test is always whether the accused will appear to take his trial.

The occasions when bail is granted include:

(i) Where a person is arrested with or without a warrant. If an arrest warrant is executed which authorises bail by being so endorsed, then bail *must* be given
(ii) Where the justices decide to remand a person on bail, rather than in custody
(iii) Where the justices, at their discretion, remand on bail accused persons who are committed for trial
(iv) Where children and young persons are involved. A person under seventeen *must* be granted bail if he cannot immediately be taken before a court. This applies unless the charge is one of homicide or some other grave crime, or unless it is in the interests of the juvenile to remove him from the association of criminals or prostitutes, or if his release would defeat the ends of justice

(v) When an accused is awaiting trial on a charge not regarded as serious

(vi) When the High Court grants bail to a person appealing to it against conviction or sentence from a court of summary jurisdiction. It may also grant bail to a person applying by way of case stated to the High Court

(vii) When the Court of Appeal (Criminal Division) grants bail pending determination of the accused's appeal. This will only occur in exceptional cases.

Surety for bail

So far as the people who stand surety are concerned, the amount of money they must be willing to forfeit if the prisoner absconds is open to complete discretion by the person granting bail, but certain people cannot act as sureties. They include:

(i) An infant (ie someone under eighteen). This is the age at which he may enter into contractual agreements

(ii) The solicitor of the defendant. This was the result of a case in 1876 (R v Scott Jervis) when it was felt that he should not do so. But this does not prevent a solicitor standing surety for a friend in a private capacity

(iii) A person who has been indemnified by the accused. Any such agreement over bail is illegal in that it tends to produce a public mischief, and the parties will be guilty of conspiracy.

In addition to these prohibitions, the standing of the person who acts as surety must be considered. Points to remember include:

(i) He must be of good character

(ii) Preferably, he should be of some substance, eg a householder

(iii) A married woman does not stand bail unless she has a separate estate (this has been possible since the Married Women's Property Act 1882)
(iv) He should not have been convicted of crime
(v) He should not be bankrupt
(vi) A prisoner cannot act as surety for a defendant because he is not able to supervise him.

Occasionally, in spite of all the precautions taken in granting bail, a person acting as bailsman gains knowledge that the accused intends to disappear, or not turn up at court. Colloquially, this is known as 'skipping bail'. He may make plans to leave the country, he may simply vanish from his usual habitat or he may employ other methods of evasion. This creates something of a problem for the surety who realises that he is going to lose his money, even though the accused may be a friend. He can, however, take steps to relieve himself of the responsibility by arresting the accused and taking him before a court, or to a police station. Written information of his suspicions to the authorities will suffice in lieu of an arrest and the police will take the necessary steps to apprehend him. Clearly, it is in the surety's interest to do this.

SEVEN
Miscellaneous Courts

THE COURT OF CHIVALRY

The Court of Chivalry is said to be the oldest secular court in the world and it deals with claims to coats of arms. It was revived as recently as 1954 in a case involving Manchester Corporation and Manchester Palace of Varieties Ltd, and in which the City of Manchester complained that the theatre was using, without authority, the city's armorial bearing. Court action was necessary to settle the dispute, but the first thing was to decide whether or not this particular court was obsolete.

The decision was made by the Earl Marshal and the Lord Chief Justice who concluded that the Court of Chivalry was still a valid court. It could only be abolished by statute and as this had not been done, it heard the case. It decided in favour of the City of Manchester, but would not prevent the use of the arms purely as a decoration, provided it was not misleading. This court itself has no power to punish, but contempt of its orders can be dealt with by Queen's Bench Division.

This case was the first time the Court of Chivalry had sat for over 200 years—three cases were heard between 1731 and 1737, and then no more until 1954. It is impossible to trace the court's origins because few records exist, although it is believed to have been constituted by Edward III. Its jurisdiction, however, embraced all matters of honour and courtesy; as it had criminal jurisdiction over knights and noblemen, it became involved with coats of arms. The most severe penalty which it could impose was degradation from the knighthood, and one of the first such punishments was meted out in 1322 upon Sir Andrew Harclay. Apparently there have been only two other such cases.

The court seems to have originated as a military court and was held before its judges who were the Lord Constable and the Earl Marshal. The Earl Marshal was commander of England's medieval armies. Its original name was Curia Militaris and its procedure was known as *secundum legem amorum*— meaning 'according to the law of arms'. A typical conflict arose in 1385 between Sir Richard de Scrope and Sir Robert Grosvenor. Scrope alleged that Grosvenor had usurped his family coat of arms and this type of conflict took the court into the realms of civil actions rather than military ones. Its advocates were civil lawyers who practised in the ecclesiastical courts and in Admiralty. Appeal lay to the king from this court.

The legal authority of this court was statutorily recognised in 1389 by the statute 13 Rich II, c 2, s 1 and its original jurisdiction over military personnel ceased in the reign of Henry VIII, almost two centuries later. It was statutorily recognised as a court martial by the Mutiny Act 1689, and today its military jurisdiction is dealt with by courts martial. Armorial work is also undertaken by the College of Arms.

COURTS LEET

In their early days these ancient courts had power to deal with breaches of the peace. In 1887, their powers were ratified by the Sheriff's Act, but since then the power of the justices has increased until it embraces almost everything done by those old courts. Nonetheless, they still exist in England, but are usually connected with common and waste land, or disputes over mineral rights. They come under varied titles such as courts of frankpledge, or courts baron, but all come under the main heading of courts leet. Apart from court leet itself, court baron is the name most frequently met with.

A court baron is a manorial court and, during the last century, it was held every three weeks in some manors. Such courts dealt chiefly with rights of land within the manors and in 1747, George III limited them to the recovery of rent and civil claims where the damages did not exceed 40s (£2). These powers were further reduced in 1833. By 1846, when the new county courts were instituted, most had fallen into disuse. Many lords of the manor therefore forfeited their rights to hold courts baron. The lords could also surrender these ancient rights, and this many of them did, and their work was transferred to the county courts. But not all the lords surrendered these rights to the Crown and so some courts baron remained. Their criminal jurisdiction is very limited, even at common law. Technically they are allowed to deal only with assaults, batteries and similar offences and could inflict a fine of 20s (£1), in default of which they could impose a prison sentence of not more than one month. In practice, these powers will never be used; their power to punish has been removed by modern legislation.

The courts leet, on the other hand, could at the outset deal with all crimes punishable at common law. All such offences were, in effect, breaches of the peace and all men were pledged for each other's good behaviour. Another function of a court leet was to appoint the petty constables for each parish and town. This was done annually by the jury of the court leet and, if none were held, the task was performed by the justices of the peace.

From 1267, prelates, peers and clergymen were exempted from attending courts leet and, in 1461, Edward IV transferred much of their power to quarter sessions. This meant a drastic reduction in their work but they continued to sit in their varied forms and do so at the present time. While the *Royal Commission on Assizes and Quarter Sessions 1966–69* recommends the abolition of some local courts, it leaves to the government the decision whether formal termination of unnamed local courts is worthwhile.

Courts leet persisted in some strange places—even within the City and Borough of Westminster a court leet persisted until well into the nineteenth century. It was convened by the High Sheriff and selected eighty householders to act as constables. Their names went before the Court of Burgesses and the constables were sworn in by that court, rather like modern policemen are sworn in by magistrates. Today there are seventy or eighty courts leet of various types in England and they administer land and property. Some are courts baron but even today all retain the power to enquire into criminal offences although they have no power to punish. In practice, they never touch criminal matters.

Existing examples are the court leet of Laxton in Nottinghamshire which determines local agricultural policy for the year; and the Great Barmote Court which supervises the lead mining in Derbyshire and which has two divisions, the Monyash court and the Wirksworth court. There is also the Dunmow Flitch, which survives from the Dunmow court which sat in the middle ages to determine the happiest married couple, who were awarded a flitch of bacon. In Ashton-under-Lyne there is a court leet which deals with road repairs, rights of way and appoints its own mayor, high constables, jurken and an aletaster. Other courts leet include the Hungerford Tutti-men, the Court of Purbeck Marblers and many more.

Occasionally, the decisions of courts leet attract the headlines. In 1966, one in Ryedale, North Riding, barricaded a farmer's road with barbed wire when he refused to pay a 17s (85p) fine which the court had imposed. Also, at Lealholm in the North Riding there is a notice on the village green dealing with rights of way, parking, etc, and which is headed 'The jury of the court leet of Danby Parish'.

Procedure is so varied, and is usually unique to one particular court, so that no attempt is made to outline it.

UNIVERSITY COURTS

The ordinary civil courts have no jurisdiction over the University of Oxford. This arises from charters by Edward III and Henry VIII which gave the university exclusive civil jurisdiction over its members.

The court which fulfils this task sits in Convocation House and is known as the Court of the Vice Chancellor. Its judge is the Assessor of the Court, and is a barrister of at least five years standing and a member of Convocation. He can be assisted by one or both of the Proctors, if they so desire, and in effect the Assessor is deputy to the Vice Chancellor. He may give leave for either party to proceed to the ordinary courts, but without such leave no other court can deal with university affairs.

The court had a very small criminal jurisdiction, but it has never been able to deal with felonies, treason and mayhem. As the Criminal Law Act 1967 abolished the distinction between felonies and misdemeanours, it now seems that this court cannot deal with any criminal offence. Advocates appear only with leave, unless they are proctors of the court, ie solicitors of the Supreme Court admitted by the Vice Chancellor. Proctors of the university must be MAs, but proctors of the Chancellor's Court need not be MAs of Oxford University.

The university court may also enquire into weights and measures in the City of Oxford, a task performed by two 'clerks of the market'.

The proceedings of the court are conducted in accordance with the law of the land, and the customs of the university. The registrar or his deputy must be present at each sitting and must make a record of the proceedings. The Vice Chancellor must appoint a Mandatory to be present at all sessions, and he acts as usher or agent and carries out the court's orders.

The court of Oxford University has sat only once between 1961 and 1969. Its sister court, the Chancellor's Court of Cambridge University, is not used at all, although its powers and jurisdiction were similar to those of Oxford's court.

THE PALATINE COURTS OF LANCASTER AND DURHAM

Palatines were independent parts of England and were partially exempt from the general laws. They were almost principalities although their judicial system closely followed that of the parent country. Their courts were bound by common law, and by the statute law of England unless it was expressly provided to the contrary. The powers of a palatine ruler were akin to those of the sovereign: he could pardon treasons and murder, he could appoint justices in eyre and justices of assize,

and all indictments or writs were in the name of the person
who owned the franchise of the particular palatinate area.

The word 'palatine' was used because there was no equivalent word in English to indicate the import of this favour, by
which the chosen person or place had royal privileges, even
though they existed within a kingdom. A county palatine was
in effect a tiny country within a larger one—a common occur-
rence on the continent in medieval times. The palatine counties of Durham and Lancaster therefore had their own courts,
although these were often staffed by judges who sat in the
royal courts. These palatine courts are represented today by
the chancery courts of the two respective counties, both being
operative. The origin of the palatine courts is as follows.

Lancaster

In 1351 Edward III granted to his cousin, the Duke of
Lancaster, a charter conferring on him the status of Count
Palatine. This particular charter, however, was valid only
during the life of the duke who died a few years later in 1361.
The palatinate therefore expired. In 1377, however, it was
revived in favour of Edward III's son, John of Gaunt, who
married the daughter of the Duke of Lancaster and who was
made duke in 1362. This palatinate also ran for his life-time, but
in 1390 a like charter was granted to the then duke and this
was extended to include his male heirs. One of them, however,
was a king—Henry VI—and because of this anomaly, the
title of Duke, or Duchess, of Lancaster has since been held by
the sovereign.

When the original charter was granted by Edward III, it
meant that the then Duke of Lancaster could hold, in his
county palatine, a chancery court presided over by the chancellor of the Duchy. The palatinate could also have its own
court of pleas, justices of oyer, terminer and gaol delivery
and justices of assize. The latter have disappeared with the
growth of the assize courts, but the chancery court remains
to this day. It has jurisdiction over the residents of the county
palatine, and its jurisdiction and powers are equal to those of
the High Court. There is right of appeal to the Court of Appeal

(Civil Division) and the jurisdiction of the Chancery Division is concurrent with that of the Palatine Court.

Today the chancellor of the Duchy of Lancaster is a politician and not a judicial officer, consequently the judicial functions of the court are undertaken by the vice chancellor. He is a barrister of at least five years standing and holds office on the same terms as a judge of the High Court. He takes precedence after them. There are three districts in the Lancaster palatinate: Liverpool, Manchester and Preston, each with their own registrar appointed by the chancellor. They perform the duties of Masters in Chancery.

When the Judicature Acts of 1873 and 1875 abolished many superior courts to form the Supreme Court, it left the chancery courts of Durham and Lancaster alone. The Lancaster court is still fairly busy—something like a hundred actions are dealt with annually. The *Royal Commission on Assizes and Quarter Sessions 1966–69* recommends that this court be reconstituted to form a branch of the High Court.

Durham

As a county palatine, Durham seems to be older than Lancaster, and it was possibly created by William the Conqueror.

With an Act of 1536, however, the independent judicial system of Durham was retained but at the same time put under the control of the king. As a small favour, the king (Henry VIII) said that the bishop of Durham and his chancellor should be ex-officio justices. In 1646, the palatinate was formally abolished and in 1654 Durham reverted to an ordinary county.

However, its local courts continued, but complaints about their actions were frequent and an Act of 1858 separated the bishop's temporal duties from his ecclesiastical ones. In 1836, the county court of the palatine was abolished but the other main courts remained. The Court of Pleas was reorganised in 1839, but through the County Courts Act 1846 which established the modern county courts, it became possible in 1875 to merge this ancient court with the newly created High Court of Justice. In spite of all these changes, the chancery court of Durham survives. Its practice was regulated in 1889 and there are appeals to the Court of Appeal (Civil Division) and to the House of Lords.

The Durham court is seldom used, and the *Royal Commission on Assizes and Quarter Sessions 1966–69* recommends its abolition.

Other counties palatine

Very few English counties ranked as counties palatine. The palatinate of Chester is said to be the most ancient, having been conferred by William I upon Hugh Lupus in 1077. It had its own courts of pleas, chancery and exchequer, but all these courts were abolished in 1830.

The fourth palatine county was Pembrokeshire in Wales, but its jurisdiction was removed as long ago as 1536 by Henry VIII. The Isle of Ely was not a palatine—merely a royal franchise.

COURT OF RECORD FOR THE HUNDRED OF SALFORD

This court was statutorily founded in 1868 by the amalgamation of the Salford Hundred Court and the Manchester Court of Record. The Salford Hundred Court dates from earlier than the Norman conquest, when it was a hundred moot. Its existence has been continuous since that time. The Manchester Court of Record, on the other hand, dates only from 1838.

The jurisdiction of the Court of Record for the Hundred of Salford is confined to civil actions where not more than £50 is claimed. This limit can be increased to £100 by the Chancellor of the Duchy of Lancaster. Its jurisdiction is akin to that of a county court, but is only valid in Manchester and Salford.

Its practice and procedure follows that of the High Court. The judge is a barrister of at least ten years standing and is assisted by a registrar. The court still sits in Manchester and there is right of appeal to the Court of Appeal (Civil Division). This is another court which the *Royal Commission on Assizes and Quarter Sessions 1966–69* recommends should be abolished.

THE LIVERPOOL COURT OF PASSAGE

This is an old local court which has survived earlier amalgamations of the civil courts.

Its jurisdiction comes partly from custom and partly from common law, although it does have a statutory foundation. Henry III, in a charter dated 24 March 1229, gave Liverpool the right to hold a portmote, although it appears that the court existed before that lawful authority. There are no records of this earlier court—they are believed to have been kept in Liverpool Town Hall but the building was damaged by fire in 1795 and records of the court were lost.

In the eighteenth century, the mayor or his deputy presided; the bailiffs and town clerk acted as registrars. In 1834 a barrister was appointed to be assistant to the mayor and his bailiffs, and in 1836 legal authority permitted him to sit alone. In 1893, the Court of Passage Act gave this person the title of 'presiding judge' and, from that time, the mayor played a diminishing role in the court's affairs. The presiding judge, however, still officially represents the Lord Mayor in court and is referred to as 'My lord'. Today, the judge must be a barrister of at least seven years standing and his appointment is part-time, like a recorder. He is assisted by a registrar.

The court was once known as the Mayor's Court but the origin of the title Court of Passage is obscure. In the middle ages, merchant ships often sailed in convoys at regular intervals and their destination was known as the *passagium*. The title probably comes from this.

The practice and procedure of this court differs only very slightly from that of the High Court, although it is inferior to it. Its jurisdiction, unless otherwise legally provided, embraces the city of Liverpool and the waters of the port of Liverpool. If an action is within the scope of the local county court, it will be dealt with there, which leaves the Court of Passage free to transact its own specialised work. There is no limit to the nature, amount or value of the cause of an action, but there is no power to serve a writ of this court outside England and Wales.

If, however, it can be shown that part of the cause of an action arose within the jurisdiction of the court, and if it exceeds £20, then leave may be granted to serve the writ out of jurisdiction. This also applies if the action is not one that can be brought in the county court, eg one of the court's own specialised cases. In actions not exceeding £20, the whole cause must have arisen within the court's jurisdiction.

This is a busy court. In 1968, for example, 1,391 writs were issued and over 1,100 of them were for claims, damages, personal injuries, negligence, etc. In the same year, the registrar disposed of 351 cases and the judge, at sittings of the court (which are held five times a year) disposed of 129 cases.

The court has a number of good points—it deals swiftly with its business and its legal charges are smaller than other courts' but in spite of this, the *Royal Commission on Assizes and Quarter Sessions 1966–69* says it should be abolished.

COURT OF PROTECTION

This is a special department of the High Court which manages the property of those who are mentally incapable of looking after their own business and affairs. It consists of the Lord Chancellor and judges of Chancery Division.

RESTRICTIVE PRACTICES COURT

This court investigates trading agreements which allegedly offend the public's interest. It consists of three High Court judges and expert assessors; there is right of appeal to the Court of Appeal (Civil Division).

TOLZEY COURT OF BRISTOL AND COURT OF PIE POWDER

This old court, which has unlimited civil jurisdiction in Bristol, is still very much alive. In practice, the recorder of Bristol is the judge, although this is not statutorily necessary.

As with so many of these ancient courts, the origins of this one are obscure. Tolzey comes from an old word meaning the guildhall or the toll-booth. It also means toll-seat or even toll-hall, and can refer to a borough courthouse. The word includes any local judicial court held in one of these places, hence the name tolzey court. Other tolzey courts once held at Gloucester and King's Lynn have ceased to exist.

Like the Liverpool Court of Passage, there are no records of the early work and foundations of the Bristol court, but the title appears in 1289 in documents in the Bristol city archives. It appears to have developed from the early court of *pied poudre* which was patronised by travelling merchants in medieval times. These words mean 'dusty feet', and it is from them that our words 'pie powder' have come. The court of pie powder runs conjointly with the tolzey court and is the only one of over seventy courts of pie powder which is still in existence.

Today, the tolzey court and the court of pie powder operate as follows: on 30 September each year the court of pie powder is opened in the Market Hall, then adjourned to the local office for fourteen days from 30 September until 13 October. The only difference between hearings in the court of pie powder and those in the tolzey court is indicated in the preamble to the proceedings. Those before the tolzey court begin with 'In the Tolzey Court of the City and County of Bristol', but if proceedings are before the court of pie powder, the words 'held in the Old Market Hall there' are added. In Bristol, there used to be a mayor's court, and a court of the stable, but these disappeared in favour of the tolzey court.

The jurisdiction of the tolzey court is rather like that of the Liverpool Court of Passage. It is an inferior court, but the jurisdiction is unlimited as to amount, although the cause of the action must arise wholly or partly within the City and County of Bristol, or the port of Bristol. All process must be served there. It is not necessary that the plaintiff shall reside in the locality, but either he, or his solicitor, must have an address within the court's jurisdiction so that process can be served. The defendant does not have to reside there—it is sufficient for him to be there, within the jurisdiction, at the time of the service of the writ or summons.

The judge must be a barrister of at least five years standing, but this work is always done by the recorder of Bristol or his deputy. The recorder is an ex-officio judge of the court and in his absence, his deputy can so act, but he must be similarly qualified. The deputy cannot try issues of law or fact, except in emergencies. The registrar, serjeants-at-mace and other officials are appointed by Bristol Corporation. The judge sits on dates fixed by him, but it must be at least four times a year. The procedure is that of the High Court, unless specifically provided otherwise, and is by writ. The court has a set of rules made in 1890, plus its own forms, although High Court forms can be adapted.

Appeal lies from the tolzey court to Queen's Bench Division, and legal aid may also be granted for actions in this court. The *Report of the Royal Commission on Assizes and Quarter Sessions 1966–69* recommends its abolition.

THE FOREST COURTS

In 1598, a writer called Manwood, in his book about forest laws, described a forest as follows:

A certain territory of woody grounds and fruitful pastures, privileged for wild beasts and fowls of the forest, chase and warren, to rest and abide in, in the safe protection of the king, for his princely delight and pleasure, which territory of ground, so privileged, is meered and bounded by unremoveable marks, either known by matter of record or else by prescription; and also replenished with wild beasts of venery and chase, and with great coverts of vert, for the succour of the said wild beasts, to have their abode in; for the preservation and continuance of which said place, together with the vert and venison, there are certain laws, privileges and officers belonging to the same, meet for that purpose, that are only proper unto a forest and not to any other place.

Reading this definition, and knowing that hunting of all kinds has long been a traditional English pastime, particularly among the landed classes, it will be appreciated that special steps were taken to preserve suitable areas, hence the law and officers of the forest. Following this logic, courts had to be created to deal with offenders.

In 1238, the royal forests were divided into two provinces—north and south—and the boundary was the River Trent. A justice was appointed for each and he appointed deputies. By the fourteenth century, the deputies did all the enquiries into the general state of the forests, the supervision of royal grants and the custody of persons who broke the forest laws.

In all forests there were four verderers who were 'gentlemen of good account, ability and living, and well learned in the laws of the forest'. They attended forest courts, checked the work of forestry officials and were responsible to the Crown. Also in each forest were four agisters who collected the money for the agistment and pannage of cattle and pigs in the king's demesne forests. There were other officials called woodwards, rangers and wardens, all of whom attended court in their particular role.

The Norman kings kept the forests for themselves and made laws to protect the wild life. Because there were so many forests, there were a lot of forest courts. The enforcement of the laws was sometimes the responsibility of the sheriff, although generally it fell upon the special forest justices and their officials, who were responsible to the general eyre.

A court of swainmote (or swanimote) existed in every forest and enquired into offences against the plant and animal life (known as vert and venison). These courts were attended by the various forest officials together with the swains who lived there. A court of swainmote originally met three times a year for business connected with agistment, pannage and fawning. Agistment means the grazing of livestock for a fee; pannage is a concession whereby cattle, etc, feed in the forest; and fawning is the breeding of beasts. Another type of court was the court of attachment. This was held every forty days by the verderers to enquire into offences against vert and venison. Its jurisdiction was small, for it could only adjudicate over small

L

trespasses to the vert—the larger ones were dealt with by general eyre. Offenders were detained or bailed to appear before the latter.

Yet another type of court was known as the inquisition; this enquired into some offences and handed the culprit to the general eyre. This later became synonymous with the swainmotes whose work was similar.

The general eyre was responsible for the supervision of forests and their laws, and came periodically to deal with reported offenders. But as the forests passed into other hands, the new owners held their own swainmotes and, by the sixteenth century, the value of the forest laws had gone. There were widespread abuses of the old laws and Manwood said, 'The forest laws are gone clean out of knowledge of most people'.

Few forest courts survived after 1632; but in 1667 the laws of the Forest of Dean were resurrected, followed in 1698 by those of the New Forest. These two forest courts survive to this day.

The Court of Swainmote and Attachment of the New Forest claims to be the oldest court of any sort in England and its constitution is as follows:

The official verderer	Appointed by the Queen
Five verderers	Elected by the commoners
Four verderers	Appointed by: the Ministry of Agriculture; the local planning authority; an organisation particularly concerned with the preservation of the countryside and its amenities; the Forestry Commission.

The court has various other officers:
The clerk to the verderers
The steward of the court
The senior agister
Three agisters.

In addition there are five commoners who act as part-time, voluntary agisters.

An elected verderer must hold at least one acre of land with common rights over the Forest and his duties are concerned with the exercise of common rights, and looking after commoners' animals. They are assisted in this work by the agisters who make regular patrols in the forest.

The court meets in public at the Verderer's Hall, Queen's House, Lyndhurst, between Southampton and Bournemouth. It must do so on at least six Mondays per year, and usually sits at 11 o'clock in the morning. When the public session is over, the court meets in private. Its functions are to protect the pasturage and turbary (the digging of turf on another's land) in the Forest.

The proceedings are opened by the senior agister who stands in the old oak dock with his right hand raised. On court days, all the agisters are dressed in green livery with black leather gaiters and gold buttons which bear the crown and stirrup symbol of the New Forest. The senior agister acts as court crier and calls:

Oyez, oyez, oyez. All manner of persons who have any presentment to make or matter or thing to do at this court of verderers, let them come forward and they shall be heard. God save the Queen.

After this solemn opening, any person may come forward to make known his grievance, and the assembly will listen. Usually, the business deals with the numbers of animals killed or injured on forestry roads, but it can try offences against its own bylaws made under the authority of various Forestry Acts dating between 1877 and 1964, and also under the Forestry Commission's bylaws made under the Forestry Act 1967.

Apart from this sort of work, the court deals with administrative matters appertaining to the forest, such as the payment of fees, proposals for new roads, telephones, car parks and a host of similar matters.

The other surviving court is the Verderer's Court of Attachment in the Forest of Dean. This does possess some criminal jurisdiction although it deals mainly with administrative matters. It is not a court of swainmote—in their original forms, courts of attachment were found in every forest and conducted a preliminary enquiry before passing offenders to the courts of swainmote. Later, however, these courts acquired their own independent jurisdiction and, in the Forest of Dean, the court of attachment has survived the court of swainmote. Today the Forest of Dean's court is not very busy because there are few animals there. It should meet every forty days but invariably adjourns through lack of business. Once a year, or thereabouts, there is a sitting when matters relating to the forest are discussed with local representatives of the Forestry Commission. Nonetheless, the old verderer's court still retains its ancient powers to try offences against the vert and venison and also all breaches of its regulations. Today the normal procedure is for the Forestry Commission to take action under its own bylaws, or to take offenders to an ordinary law court.

Since the seventeenth century, this court has met at Speech House in the heart of the Forest; there are four verderers and this number has persisted since their foundation in Canute's time (1016–35).

One important reason for the disappearance of this sort of court was the growth of game laws which created poaching offences; these are dealt with in the ordinary law courts, usually at magistrates' courts. The *Report of the Royal Commission on Assizes and Quarter Sessions 1966–69* makes no specific recommendations for these courts.

ECCLESIASTICAL COURTS

Many abbots were also lords of the manor and this gave them power to hold manorial courts, but their dual role sometimes caused serious complications. As lord of the manor an abbot (or an abbess) could be asked to hang felons, but as a priest he was morally bound to give sanctuary to a fleeing criminal. This penalty of death was given statutory sanction when, between 958 and 975, Edgar bestowed a charter upon

Glastonbury Abbey which gave the abbot the power to try and hang thieves. It also laid down that if the abbot or any of his monks found someone being put to death, they had to order the execution to stop.

At that time, priests were among the few people who could read or write and they had a good knowledge of canon law. It was logical that this knowledge, plus their spiritual power over wrongdoers, made them ideal to staff and administer the early courts. Their influence resulted in England being divided into provinces, dioceses, archdeaconries and rural deaneries. The archbishops of Canterbury and York presided over their own provinces in their Provincial Courts. A bishop held a diocesan court and the archdeacon dealt with administrative matters.

Because priests could read and write, they were first employed in the normal courts, but William I gave them their own ecclesiastical courts quite distinct from the general judicial system. These became known either as spiritual courts, or courts Christian, and dealt with everything, civil and criminal. Many legal systems are founded upon the early ecclesiastical courts, for example, those which deal with matrimonial affairs, including divorce. These subjects were catered for in the ecclesiastical courts until 1873 when the Judicature Act removed them, but let the ecclesiastical courts cope with matters involving the church and clergy.

The lowest of the ecclesiastical courts was the archdeacon's court, now obsolete. Its function was chiefly one of morals; it heard complaints of adultery or blasphemy and as a punishment could impose a penance or perhaps a fine. There was a right of appeal to the bishop's court.

Bishops' courts

The bishops' courts dealt with slander, and punished by fines or penances such as going to church to apologise, or wearing a slanderer's placard. The power of the church courts to deal with defamation ended in 1855 chiefly because these powers had never been used. A bishop's court also dealt with breaches of contract by enforcing the repayment of small debts upon pain of excommunication. These acts became known as breaches of faith. Excommunication was a powerful threat because it outlawed a member of the church and banned him from the sacraments; it was abolished in 1963. In addition to these powers, the bishops had their own prisons and officials, although they lost their power to execute. Even so, they could pass a convicted person to the sheriff for execution.

The power to try persons for offences against religion still exists in the ecclesiastical courts, but is never used because the church no longer feels it appropriate to place its lay members on trial for such matters.

The bishop's court was also known as the Consistory Court, but as the bishop was sometimes called the 'ordinary', this particular court was also known as the Court of the Ordinary. Its judges were drawn from lawyers at universities, known as chancellors or officials, and their training was in Roman law, or canon law. There was right of appeal from this court to the archbishop's court.

Some of the cases heard by the London Consistory Court between 1480 and 1639 included rape, incest, adultery, sorcery, bad behaviour in church, absence from mass, marital cases, telling tales and even hunting on a Sunday. A modern case appeared in 1951 before the Southwark Consistory Court when three ladies objected to a wrought-iron statue of the madonna and child. This was for display at the Festival of Britain, but before the event the vicar of St Mary-le-Park, Battersea wanted to keep the statue in his church. The ladies objected on the grounds that it was unchristian, repulsive and blasphemous. The Consistory Court heard the case and the chancellor inspected the statue, but declared it was not as they claimed. The vicar got permission to keep it in his church.

In Canterbury, the Consistory Court is known as the Commissary Court and its president is the Commissary General.

The latest reforms of ecclesiastical courts came in 1963, and the consistory court now holds jurisdiction over:

(i) Charges against the clergy for offences other than those involving doctrine, ritual or ceremonial

(ii) Faculty suits
(iii) Disputes about rights of patronage
(iv) Proceedings for penalties under some provisions of the Pluralities Act 1838 (ie section 32 says that every spiritual person shall keep residence on his benefice and in the house of residence belonging thereto).

There are penalties for disobedience, but this court has no jurisdiction over the laity.

Proceedings may be instituted by six or more persons on the electoral roll of a parish or district, against an incumbent, stipendiary curate or curate. Any person authorised by the bishop can take proceedings against a priest or deacon, and an incumbent can proceed against a stipendiary curate.

Proceedings begin with a written complaint which is laid before the diocesan registrar. The bishop interviews both parties before deciding whether to let the matter drop or to begin an enquiry. If he decides on an enquiry, an examiner will be appointed from a panel of barristers and solicitors and he begins by deciding whether there is a case for the accused to answer. During this preliminary investigation, all parties may be represented or assisted by friends or advisers.

If the examiner finds there is a case to answer, a person nominated by the bishop will promote the complaint in the consistory court. The case is heard by the chancellor who sits with four assessors (two priests and two laymen). There is right of appeal to the next senior court which is the archbishop's court.

Archbishops' courts

In York the Archbishop's court is known as the Chancery court, and in Canterbury as the Court of Arches. Each is composed of five judges of which one is a single chief justice for both courts. He is appointed by the Archbishops of Canterbury and York, acting jointly, and with the queen's approval. In Canterbury he is known as the Dean of Arches, and in York as the Auditor, although he is the same person. The other four judges comprise two laymen experienced in judicial matters and two persons in holy orders who are appointed by the Lower House of Convocation. The Court of Arches first sat in 1297, and a recent decision was reached there in April 1970, the first appeal to this ancient court since the Ecclesiastical Jurisdiction Measure 1963.

In their early days, the archbishops' courts dealt mainly with testamentary matters, such as assets left by a deceased person. They did hear appeals from the bishops' courts and, until the Reformation, there was further right of appeal to the Papal Curia. When the English sovereign became head of the reformed church, however, this type of appeal was handed over in 1558 to the Court of Delegates which consisted of leading churchmen. By the eighteenth century it was made up of common law judges and lay persons. In 1832, the jurisdiction of the Court of Delegates was passed to the Judicial Committee of the Privy Council which remains the final court of appeal in ecclesiastical law. So far as archbishops' courts are concerned, they still hear appeals from the consistory courts by clergymen who have been charged with offences against ecclesiastical law. In faculty suits, however, such an appeal will be heard only if doctrinal, ritualistic or ceremonial matters are involved, and there is further appeal in such faculty suits to the Judicial Committee of the Privy Council.

In 1963, the Ecclesiastical Jurisdiction Measure instituted a new court of Ecclesiastical Causes Reserved, mainly to hear matters not involving doctrinal, ritual or ceremonial matters. This court has original and appellate jurisdiction; it has five judges, two of whom must hold, or have held, high judicial office; and three who are, or have been, diocesan bishops. The judges are appointed by the queen and must be communicants. Decisions of this court may be reviewed by a Commission of Review appointed by the sovereign. This consists of three Lords of Appeal, and two lords spiritual of Parliament. For doctrinal matters, it can be assisted by advisers such as bishops or theologians, and is not bound by any decision of the Judicial Committee of the Privy Council on matters of doctrine, ritual or ceremonial.

Barristers and solicitors may argue a cause in an ecclesiastical court, and legal aid is available. In the event of a clergy-man being found guilty by either a consistory court, or the court of Ecclesiastical Causes Reserved, spiritual punishment will be pronounced.

It may take the following forms:

(i) A rebuke
(ii) Monition (to refrain from some specific act)
(iii) Suspension (from a duty or right)
(iv) Inhibition (disqualification from clerical functions)
(v) Deprivation (removal from preferment, and disqualification from holding any future preferment—ie 'unfrocked').

Excommunication was abolished in 1963.

The church and the state

Since the sixteenth century, the ecclesiastical courts have been losing their power. Prior to 1533, the laws of the church consisted of common law and the laws of the Roman Catholic Church, known as canon law, reinforced by various synods. After that time, the Reformation and the foundation and growth of the Church of England, altered much of the existing canon law. The changes began with the Submission of the Clergy Act, 1533. Oddly enough, the ecclesiastical law of this country binds everyone, whether members of the Church of England or not, and whether clerical or not. In this respect, it resembles that ancient canon law.

There is, however, a set of rules binding only on the clergy. These are made by convocations, ie gatherings of the clergy held in each province, and have continued since 1533. In 1603, 141 rules were made by a convocation in Canterbury province, but a judicial decision in 1736 said that rules made by these convocations were not binding on the laity.

Alterations to these rules, known as canons, have been made over the centuries; in 1964, twenty-eight new canons and one repealing canon were published to ratify the Church of England's position as the established church. Through this, it has legal authority in the State and the queen, as head of the State, is also head of the Church of England. She has supreme power over all persons in all causes, whether civil or ecclesiastical, and the law of England says the sovereign can do no wrong. This is similar to the pope's authority over members of his church, for in matters appertaining to his church, he is infallible.

In addition to the sovereign's power, certain bishops have the right to sit in the House of Lords, as the supreme court in the land. They are the Archbishops of Canterbury and York: the bishops of London, Durham, Winchester and twenty-one other senior bishops. The legislation produced by the church has the effect of a statute and, although the church has its own courts to administer its laws, the state courts supersede them and prevent them from abusing their powers.

THE TRIAL OF THE PYX

The Trial of the Pyx has been held regularly since the twelfth century, but the 1969 trial was the first to concern itself with decimal coins. The ancient procedure is a trial of the quality of our coinage and, in May 1969, a jury of twenty-four freemen of the goldsmiths company reported on the weight, fineness and composition of the coinage in accordance with the Trial of the Pyx Order, 1969.

There seems to be some doubt as to the precise origin of this quaint trial, although there was apparently a Trial of the Pyx in 1140. The earliest recorded trial, however, was in 1248 during the reign of Henry II, and the first writ to direct a trial was issued in 1281. In 1248, a jury of twelve 'discreet and lawful citizens of London with twelve skilful goldsmiths of the same place' officiated at a trial before the Barones of Exchequer. The name barone is used instead of judge, for the barones were law court judges. The venue of the trials was originally the Pyx Chamber at Westminster Abbey, but it was moved to the Mint in 1843 and finally to Goldsmiths Hall in 1870.

Over the years, the procedure has barely changed. Every

year, two Lords Commissioners sign warrants, under their authority from the Coinage Acts and these state the day of the trial and summon the jurors. On the appointed date the officials assemble at the Goldsmiths Hall in readiness for their duty. In former times the sovereign himself occasionally attended, but the general rule was that the Lord Chancellor, the Lord Treasurer, the Chancellor of the Exchequer and other members of the King's Council presided at the trial. This ended in 1870 when the Coinage Act laid down that the King's Remembrancer should preside and this has been the case ever since. Even the Privy Council itself was summoned to the Trial of the Pyx until well after 1660.

Today the gathering consists of the Queen's Remembrancer, the deputy Master of the Mint and other Mint officials, plus some officials from the Board of Trade. The Chancellor of the Exchequer still attends in his ex-officio capacity of Master of the Mint. In addition there is the jury of freemen from the Worshipful Company of Goldsmiths. They take a prominent part in the trial and belong to one of the oldest of the livery companies of the City of London. They have attended these trials since the time of Elizabeth I and their assay master comes along with them. The company has had responsibility for the quality of gold and silver used in commerce and coinage for several centuries, and freedom of the company can be gained only by apprenticeship or by patrimony. The Remembrancer wears his ceremonial dress of black lace gown, lace stock, full-bottomed wig and velvet court suit.

In the fourteenth century, the trial was held every three months and the coins had a 'privy' mark to show the period in which they were minted. Edward VI altered the period to one year, but Elizabeth I reverted to the three months for her Trials of the Pyx. After Elizabeth, however, there would be a trial occasionally whenever the pyx was full, but in 1868 the interval was fixed at five years. With the coming into force of the Coinage Act 1870, however, it was finally settled to an annual event.

The pyx is a box into which samples of coins produced by the Royal Mint are placed. The word *pyx* comes from the

Greek, meaning box. Today several pyxes are used to contain samples of all coins minted in the previous year. Each days production at the Mint was divided into specific numbers or weights. These were called 'journeys' and today the Mint is obliged to put aside one gold coin out of every 2,000 minted, one silver coin from every 150, and one cupro-nickel coin out of every 10,000 made. Officials of the Board of Trade fulfil their duties by making standard trial pieces in gold or silver, as well as scales which are accurate to the 800,000th part of a grain. In addition they produce the necessary balances and weights.

On the date of the Trial of the Pyx, the coins on trial are taken by armoured car to the Goldsmiths Hall where they are counted and checked for weight. In 1969, the new decimal coins were included. The coins, contained in the pyxes, plus the trial pieces and the standards, are handed over to the jury who carry out their careful and ancient duty during the next few weeks. They assay the samples to see if they are correct in weight and fineness, and the opening procedure takes place in private.

The jurors take an oath to:

> . . . well and truly make the assays of these moneys of gold and silver and truly report the said moneys to be in fineness and weight according to the standard weights for weighing and testing the coins of the realm, and the standard trial plates of gold and silver used for determining the justness of the gold and silver coinage of the realm in the custody of the Board of Trade.

In 1969 they swore to 'truly report if the said moneys were in weight, fineness or composition in conformity with the Decimal Currency Act 1967'.

The metal of the coins is compared with pieces taken from four standard trial plates of gold, silver, copper and nickel, and the gold coins may be melted down for this purpose. It is only the gold coins, and the silver Maundy Money which can nowadays be truly compared against the standard plates.

The trial always begins in February, and the entire court re-assembles in May to hear the verdict. This is given by the Queen's Remembrancer and records show that no faults have been found within living memory. When it is all over, and the verdict is duly recorded, those who took part in the trial indulge in a custom which dates from the seventeenth century —they go and have a meal.

EIGHT
Obsolete Courts

CURIA REGIS

One early court was the Curia Regis. The words mean Royal Council but also referred to a place where the king lived and was attended by his court or his household. It was the supreme central court where all government business was done.

Before Norman times, there was no true legal system and the law was administered by the king and his council. It was William I who established this, the King's Court, known sometimes as the Aula, but more commonly as the Curia Regis. The king himself attended and so did all his chief officers of state. It included all the officials who lived at the palace, plus anyone nominated by the king and it included all his tenants-in-chief —the lords, in other words.

The Curia Regis accompanied the king on all his travels, and it even went overseas to the dominions, adjudicating on disputes and dispensing justice wherever it went. In this respect, it had unlimited jurisdiction and dealt with many public problems of every type. These were legal, administrative and judicial—in fact, everything to do with running a country. Civil and criminal matters came under its wing even though the members of the council possessed no particular legal knowledge or qualifications. Membership of the council was unpaid and regarded as an honour, but it committed its members to a lot of hard work, and some expense.

When all its members were present, the Curia Regis was known as the Great Council, but it only met like this on the most important occasions. From it grew our modern legislature, including Parliament (see page 17). It consisted of the most important people in the land. There were the Lord Chancellor, the Lord Treasurer, the Lord Privy Seal, the Lord President of the King's Council, some principal judges and certain bishops and barons. Before the Court of King's Bench was established, the Council heard appeals and for this task some forty of its members sat. It heard appeals from the Court of Common Pleas which later developed into the system whereby appeals were channelled through King's Bench Division to the House of Lords.

In time, though, the Curia Regis became too large to operate efficiently. It undertook so many duties that its variety of tasks became a problem and gradually it split into separate departments, each dealing with some aspect of its overall work. From these have grown the Cabinet, the Privy Council, the Law Courts and various ministries in Whitehall.

In the twelfth century there developed a department to deal with financial matters and this was staffed by men known as barones. It later became known as the exchequer, and the early courts of exchequer (see page 181) were staffed by judges known as barons (the letter 'e' of barones was dropped). The establishment of the Court of Exchequer was perhaps the first court of common law, and its work involved litigants who sought redress because of pressure to pay debts when they themselves were owed money.

GENERAL EYRE

Meanwhile, the General Eyre was travelling the country. This was also a division of the Curia Regis and consisted of judges who travelled to dispense justice. They were appointed by the king and operated on his behalf and in his name. They took their work seriously, but had little or no legal knowledge, and many were nothing more than clerks who had served in the King's Court at Westminster. By the reign of Richard I (1189–99) members of the General Eyre were chosen from ecclesiastics who knew a little about the law, simply through service in the courts of Exchequer and Chancery.

The eyres were irregular; theoretically they were to visit each place at least once every seven years, but more often the interval was longer. The result was that prisoners awaiting trial never knew when to expect the eyre and often had to wait years. In 1321, an eyre was held in the Tower of London forty years after the previous visit!

Some weeks prior to its arrival, officials came with a questionaire for the sheriff to complete. It had to show the business to be conducted before the forthcoming eyre and these statements were known as articles of eyre; generally they provided a source of finance for the king. The detection of crime was a source of revenue because convicted felons forfeited their property. Other topics decided by the eyre might concern Jews, fugitives, widows, treasure trove, weights and measures, marriages, customs, crime and a host of other items. The sheriff had to answer questions and had to report his actions since the previous eyre. He had to make sure that all orders had been obeyed because the eyre would inspect his records, together with those of the coroner and the judges, to make sure everything had been done. An official who took over from someone else was deemed responsible for all errors, no matter how old they might be. Because of their severity, the eyres were hated by everyone. In 1223, it was announced that an eyre would visit Cornwall and all the people concerned fled; in 1261, the populace of Worcester refused to have anything to do with the eyre on the grounds that it was over seven years since the previous one.

There was another problem—anyone wishing to appeal to the eyre never knew where it was, and they began to ask the barones of Exchequer to settle their problems. These officials were more amenable than the justices of the eyres. Eventually, through the provisions of Magna Carta, a permanent court was established so that people could come any time with their pleas. Obviously, the barones of Exchequer were dealing with pleas which were not strictly within their jurisdiction and, when the permanent court was established at Westminster Hall, all such claims went there.

COURT OF COMMON PLEAS

The first court to be based at Westminster Hall was the Court of Common Pleas. This arose through Magna Carta's insistence on having a court at a settled place and Common Pleas was England's first law court. It was an off-shoot of the Curia Regis. A chief justice of common pleas was appointed and given power to hear and determine all civil causes between the king's subjects. Initially, he remained at Westminster while the king and his court travelled the countryside, and this judge heard cases involving claims to land, trespass to persons and property, debt and other problems. Trespass on land, which was regarded as something very personal, was not dealt with.

The Court of Common Pleas became very busy. For one thing, the early members of the legal profession found themselves making a considerable amount of money from people with claims—this type of work paid better than criminal matters.

THE ROYAL COURTS OF JUSTICE

Eventually, other courts became settled in a particular place, and because Westminster Hall was large enough to accommodate them, they all found a home there. King's Bench was there, and so were the courts of Exchequer and Chancery, plus a few more. Westminster Hall therefore became the first site of England's Royal Courts of Justice.

The king sometimes attended the Westminster court, but not always; the early records show whether or not he was present by the inscriptions upon them. Those marked *coram regis* mean 'before the king', while those marked *coram justiciares de banco* mean 'before the justices of the bench'.

Many historic events took place there. Charles I was condemned before seventy judges; Oliver Cromwell became Lord Protector; Guy Fawkes was tried and so was Sir Thomas More. In 1517, 480 men and eleven women appeared on a joint

M

charge of riot and assault, and the king turned up to watch this case.

The very last case to be tried at Westminster Hall ended on 28 December 1882. It was a libel case, and it marked the end of Westminster Hall as the home of the Royal Courts of Justice. In the 1920s it was used as an overflow from the newly built courts in the Strand, but, by virtue of the Judicature Act 1873 which became operative in 1875, the courts of Common Pleas, Exchequer and King's Bench were all united to become the Supreme Court of Judicature in England. Its more popular name is the High Court of Justice.

THE COURT OF REQUESTS

This was regarded as a minor court of equity and operated in Tudor times due to an increase of the work of the Council and of Chancery. It undertook a small amount of criminal work and tried offences like forgery and riot, although it was chiefly a civil court. It was used by the poor for their civil claims and operated at roughly the same time as the Star Chamber. In many respects its jurisdiction ran on parallel lines; it might even have been a division of the Court of Star Chamber (see page 179).

The Court of Requests was statutorily recognised in 1493 and in 1529 it is on record that 'hereafter folowe the names of such counsaillours as be appoynted for the heryng of poor mennes causes in the kynges courte of requestes'. The court was initially moveable, but eventually it became static and joined the others at Westminster Hall.

The appellants at this court were invariably poor and could not afford to sue at common law; some were even the king's own servants. The judges were known as Masters of Requests and were trained at either Oxford or Cambridge in Roman and canon law. They were judges or barristers who practised in the Admiralty or the ecclesiastical courts and sat in this court as a favour to the poor. Sometimes they were asked to sit in the Star Chamber.

The Courts of Requests was irregular because its judges

could earn higher fees elsewhere; therefore attempts were made to standardise its procedure and at the same time not encroach upon the jurisdiction of the Court of Star Chamber. It was also desirable to establish permanent officials for the Court of Requests. All this was done, but it defeated the objects of the court. Its fees became higher than poor appellants could afford, but it continued to function in spite of other new and bigger courts.

In 1598, as the result of a case Stepney v Flood, the Court of Requests was declared illegal. This meant it had no power to imprison for contempt of its orders but it functioned nonetheless and gained wide support. Although it served a most useful purpose, it had never been statutorily founded and attempts were made to put it on a legal basis. This did not succeed and, after 1641, there was no procedure by which the court could legally function.

It sat for another year until 1642, and although Masters of Requests continued to be appointed, they could not fulfil any judicial duties. The next nail in the coffin was put there when the Court of Common Pleas and Queen's Bench Division forbade the taking of cases to this old court and so it became valueless. Charles II was asked to reinstate it, but felt it was of no use and so in August 1642 the Court of Requests came to an end. Its work was passed to Chancery.

COURT OF STAR CHAMBER

This old court supposedly got its name from the room used in the old Palace of Westminster for meetings of the King's Council. In 1347, during Edward III's reign, a chamber was built on the east side of the palace yard at Westminster. This was used by the council in 1348, and was then known as the 'sterred chamber'; it was not built as a court, but as a meeting place for the council. The ceiling was studded with gilded stars and one authority says the name comes from 'starra', after the Jewish covenants deposited there.

The Council used this room long before Henry VII introduced his *Pro Camera Stellata* (Star Chamber Act) 1487. This statute is sometimes given credit for the foundation of this court, but this seems wrong. The Act merely gave the existing court some additional powers; it could now examine and punish offenders as if they had been convicted by normal legal process. This meant it was a court in its own right. The Act named it as the Court of the Star Chamber, but it could only punish and try misdemeanours. It could not deal with the more serious offences, known as felonies, and could not therefore inflict the death penalty. Nonetheless, it won an evil reputation, for it administered cruelties and torture. Many felt it abused the spirit of Magna Carta in both criminal and civil cases because it did not conform to the rules of law.

There were two procedures in this court. One was known as *ore tenus*—by the mouth, and the other was by *bill and answer*. The first often took place through secret information given to the council and from which an accused could be taken before them. He could be privately examined, without the oath, and if he did not answer he was sent to prison until he changed his mind. Sometimes an accused was tricked into saying something which the court accepted as a confession and if he did this, he was taken into the court where his confession was read out. He was then convicted *ex ore suo*—out of his own mouth.

The second procedure—*bill and answer*—meant that a Bill, produced upon the Attorney General's information, led to the accused being served with a writ containing the charge against him. He had to write an answer after which he was summoned before the court. There he was forced to answer, on oath, a written interrogation. The oath was very similar to a modern one, but the method of interrogation was brutal. Torture was used to make the witnesses tell the 'truth' and, when all the evidence had been presented, the council deliberated and produced a verdict of guilty or innocent, without a jury.

The offences dealt with by this court varied a great deal although it could not deal with capital offences and, at that time, a multitude of offences carried the death penalty. But the Court of Star Chamber called such offences high misdemeanours and omitted all reference to the word felony. This meant it dealt with all kinds of offence and could deliver every kind of penalty except death. Imprisonment, fines, branding, mutilation and the pillory were imposed, and the offences included riots, conspiracy, libel, attempted murder, coinage offences, burglary, blackmail and various frauds.

In many respects, the Court of Star Chamber did a service to modern criminal law by creating these offences, which, as it was not a common law court, it could do by making its own rules. Many of these offences exist today, some in the form of common law misdemeanours and others in statute form. Modern legislation owes a lot to this cruel but wise old court.

In spite of its work, it was to disappear. Charles I abolished it by statute in 1641 and most of its work was thereafter done by King's Bench Division.

EXCHEQUER COURT

Tradition says that Henry VIII had the royal nurseries over the Exchequer Court in Westminster Hall, the original home of the Royal Courts of Justice. The Exchequer Court dealt mainly with matters of royal or public revenue. It stems from the division of the Curia Regis when departments were established to cope with all the latter's responsibilities and was the first common law court to divide itself from the royal courts.

To ease their burden of work, the royal courts created an exchequer with a treasurer in charge. This was not a court; it was an office to deal with revenue. But as the work was so akin to the law, the exchequer soon found itself acting as a court by deciding common pleas. People came with financial problems and, if possible, the exchequer decided the issue for them. Important men who had presided over the Curia Regis now sat in the exchequer, and the judicial side of their work became known as the Exchequer of Pleas. For a time, in the thirteenth century, it decided all manner of pleas, most of them totally unconnected with money, but this practice was quickly stopped and it concentrated on common pleas connected with revenue until its abolition.

Eventually it settled down into an acceptable form and consisted of three or four revenue officials, known as barones, who had no connection with the nobility. The word meant male officials. Its work grew until it divided into two parts—legal and administrative. The legal section, with the barones in charge, travelled on circuit from the time of Elizabeth I and this made it like any other court with travelling judges. From 1585, the judges used the exchequer chamber for their work.

There was appeal from the Court of Exchequer Pleas to a court set up in 1357 as a court of error from the Exchequer. It consisted of the Lord Chancellor and Lord Treasurer, but in 1589 the chief justices of Queen's Bench Division and the Common Pleas were given power to act as delegates. This court was abolished in 1830, after which appeal was to the House of Lords.

The Court of Exchequer ended in 1842 when its jurisdiction was transferred to the Chancery Division of the High Court.

Short Glossary Of Legal Terms

Abet	To encourage and assist in the commission of an offence.
Abjure	To leave the realm for ever. Once used in lieu of death sentence.
Acquit	To discharge from financial liability or from a criminal charge. To set free.
Act of Parliament	Law made by the sovereign in Parliament. There are various kinds, eg local, personal, public, general, private.
Action	Taking civil proceedings to demand one's lawful rights.
Adjourn	To suspend or put off a hearing until later. Adjourned *sine die* means to suspend for an indefinite period.
Admission	A confession, written or oral, used in evidence.
Advocate	A person who pleads for another in court, ie barrister or solicitor.
Affidavit	Written statement on oath, sworn before any person authorised to administer oaths.
Amercement	'At the mercy' of the lord (appertaining to local courts). A fine.
Appeal	A complaint to a higher court

	that injustice has been done, plus a request that it be rectified.
Appellate jurisdiction	The jurisdiction of a court which hears apeals.
Arraign	To call an accused person to the bar of the court. To answer a charge.
Arrest	To deprive a person of his liberty.
Autrefois acquit *Autrefois convict* }	(another time acquitted; another time convicted). A plea that a person has already been tried and dealt with for the offence in question, and either been acquitted or convicted.
Bar	(i) The place in court where prisoners are tried (ii) The place occupied by barristers in court to speak for clients; hence 'barrister' (iii) The profession of barrister; barristers collectively.
Bench	Judges of a law court; justices of a magistrate's court; bishops in the House of Lords.
Bill	Bill in Parliament—a measure prior to being made law and submitted to both Houses of Parliament.
Bind over	To order a person to enter into a recognizance to do, or to abstain from doing, a specified act—ie to keep the peace.
Black cap	A square cap, forming part of the judges' robes. Worn over the wig on ceremonial occasions and when passing the death sentence.

Bona fide	In good faith; honestly.
Bote	Compensation; to make amends.
Breach of the peace	The queen's peace, or shortly, the peace, is the normal state of society which exists. Any interruption of that peace and good order is a breach of the peace.
Canon	A rule, especially of ecclesiastical law.
Capital punishment	The death penalty.
Cause	A legal action; that which results in a legal action.
Caveat	Warning (means 'let him beware'). A legal notice to stop or remove civil proceedings, especially in the Probate, Divorce and Admiralty Division; to prevent an executor proving a will.
Certiorari	(means 'to be more fully informed of'). An order issued by a high court to an inferior court to remove proceedings to a superior court for further consideration.
Chambers	Rooms used by a judge to deal with business when an open court hearing is unnecessary.
Charge	A criminal accusation.
Circumstantial evidence	Evidence, not of the actual fact to be proved, but other facts from which that fact may be presumed with more or less certainty.
Codicil	A documentary addition to an existing will; an appendix.
Common law	Ancient unwritten laws of the kingdom; general customs regarded as law since time immemorial.
Complaint	The setting in motion of civil proceedings in a magistrates' court;

an application to a justice upon which he has the authority to make an order for the payment of money or otherwise.

Contract	A legally enforceable agreement.
Cross-examination	Examination of a witness by the opposition after his initial examination.
De facto	In fact.
De jure	By right.
De minimus non curat lex	The law does not concern itself with trifling matters.
De novo	Anew.
Decree absolute	Divorce court order to dissolve or annul a marriage.
Decree nisi	Provisional order to dissolve or annul a marriage.
Defendant	Person sued in a civil court; person charged in a criminal court.
Demesne	A manor house with lands attached (domain).
Deodand	A personal chattel which had caused death to anyone, and therefore forfeited to the Crown.
Deposition	Statement made on oath before a justice, taken down in writing in the presence and hearing of the accused and read over to, and signed by, the person making it, and by the justice.
Easement	Rights over another's property.
Estop	To stop; procedure to prevent denial of a fact already admitted.
Estreat	To levy fines; copy of a document relating to fines.
Evidence	The term used to indicate the means by which any fact or point in issue or question may be proved

	or disproved in a manner complying with the legal rules governing the subject.
Ex gratia	As a favour.
Ex-officio	By virtue of an office; jurisdiction held by someone because of their office.
Examination	Putting questions to a witness.
Eyre	Judges on circuit; forerunner of assizes.
Faculty	Privilege, permission or favour granted to by-pass common law rules, ie to marry without banns. Leave by a consistory court to alter the fabric of a church or erect memorials, etc.
Felony	Serious criminal offence, once involving forfeiture of goods. Abolished in 1968.
First instance, court of	A court before which an action, civil or criminal, is first tried.
Franchise	A privilege given by the sovereign or the government.
Garnishee	A person who is warned (garnished), ie forbidden to pay a debt to a creditor; instead he pays someone who has obtained final judgement against the creditor.
Habeas Corpus	A writ ordering someone to 'have the body' taken before a court, ie to produce a prisoner unlawfully held. (Historically used to prevent unlawful imprisonment).
Hearsay evidence	Evidence of what a witness has heard another person, not the defendant, say. Second-hand evidence.

Homicide	The killing of a human being by a human being.
Impeachment	A serious criminal accusation before the House of Lords by the House of Commons. The arraignment of a peer or minister of state for treason or maladministration.
In camera	In private.
In curia	In open court.
Indict	(pronounced indite). To charge with a crime; to accuse.
Indictment	(pronounced inditement). A written or printed accusation setting out a serious crime against one or more persons for which they may be tried by a jury. It is made on behalf of the sovereign and is read to them at their trial, before the plea.
Infanticide	Where a woman by any wilful act or omission causes the death of her child being under the age of twelve months, but, at the time of such act or omission, the balance of her mind was disturbed by reason of

(i)   not having fully recovered from the effects of childbirth, or

(ii) the effects of lactation.

Information	A verbal or written charge made before a justice to the effect that some person has committed an offence or act for which he is liable to be punished.
Injunction	A civil court order to refrain from

a non-criminal act. A mandatory injunction requires a person to do some specified thing.

Instrument A formal legal document.

Interlocutory order Intermediate order; not final. One which does not include a case, eg an order to inspect documents.

Interpleader An application for relief from claims, ie where two claimants each require the same person to pay the same debt, and there is doubt as to which is the true claimant. Discussion of an incidental point.

Judgement Decision of a court or a judge.

Jurisdiction The limits of legal authority or power which can be exercised, ie by a court, a judge, a magistrate, etc.

Lay Non-ecclesiastical, or the opposite of professional.

Leading questions Those which suggest the answer; can be answered generally by 'yes' or 'no'.

Legatee Someone to whom a legacy is bequeathed.

Libel Defamatory words in writing.

Mandamus (we command). An order issued by a superior court to compel a person or court to do some duty.

Manslaughter The unlawful killing of a human being by a human being without malice, eg a sudden and involuntary killing.

Mayhem Violent deprivation of a member proper for one's defence, ie losing eyes, legs, arms, etc. To maim.

Misdemeanour	Generally, an indictable offence. At one time something less than a felony.
Moot	A court; a plea; a debate. Place where moot cases were decided was a moot hall.
Murder	The unlawful killing of a human being by a human being with malice aforethought, either expressed or implied.
Nisi prius	A civil trial before a high court judge at the assizes. The words mean 'unless before' and come from the days when such a trial was held at Westminster *unless* it had taken place *before* in the county before justices of assize. *Nisi prius* business was additional to the main work of the assizes.
Not proven	A verdict of a Scottish criminal trial. Neither guilty nor not guilty. Not used in England.
Obiter dictum	Something said by a judge, not relevant to the case before him.
Onus probandi	The burden or onus of proof.
Oyer and terminer	(meaning 'to hear and determine'). A commission to judges to try offences.
Parol	By word of mouth; spoken.
Pathologist	Medical expert of diseases. One who examines dead bodies to ascertain the cause of death.
Perjury	In judicial proceedings, the making of a false statement on oath. The statement must be material to the matter before the court.
Petition	The seeking of a remedy through the civil courts, especially in

	Chancery and Divorce Divisions.
Petty sessions	The sitting of two or more magistrates in a petty sessional court house. A magistrates' court.
Plaint	The cause of an action stated by a plaintiff and entered as the commencement of an action in the books of a county court.
Plaintiff	Anyone seeking relief via civil court proceedings.
Plea	An answer to a charge in court; defendant's answer to a plaintiff's action, or to the prosecution.
Plurality	Having two, three or more benefices. A clergyman having more than one living is a pluralist.
Post mortem	(means 'after death'). The medical examination of a corpse to discover the cause of death.
Preamble	Explanatory introduction to a statute.
Prefer	To bring a charge, eg to prefer a charge of assault.
Private Bills	Bills brought into Parliament by interested individuals with a view to having them made law.
Privilege	That granted to someone beyond the ordinary course of the law, eg a priest is privileged by *practice* (not law) in that he need not disclose to a court something told to him under the seal of confession. Discussions between a lawyer and client, or a husband and wife (during marriage) are absolutely privileged. *Legally* a priest could be made to divulge a confession.

Probation	The placing by a court of a guilty person under supervision for a specified period. Supervision is by a probation officer.
Process	Documents relating to judicial proceedings; the various writs used in the course of an action, or steps taken prior to criminal proceedings. The service of a summons.
Prosecutor	(female: prosecutrix). A person who institutes or conducts judicial proceedings in an English court of criminal law.
Puisne	(pronounced pewney). Means junior. Judges of the high court other than the heads of the divisions are *puisne* judges, ie judges of a lesser rank.
Queen's evidence *(King's evidence)*	Evidence for the Crown. To turn queen's evidence is to confess guilt and become a witness against one's accomplices or colleagues.
Quid pro quo	A consideration; giving something of value in exchange for something of equal value.
R	Abbreviated form of Rex or Regina (king or queen). Used in case law, eg R v Brown (the Crown versus Brown).
Rape	(i) The unlawful sexual intercourse of a female against her will by force, fear or fraud (ii) A division of a county (iii) Violent trespass of a forest.
Realty	Real estate; land and things forming part of land.

Rebut	To oppose by argument; to prove otherwise.
Referee	Someone to whom a question is put for his decision or opinion. An arbitrator.
Regicide	The murder or murderer of a king (eg those responsible for the execution of Charles I were 'the Regicides').
Remand	To order that a defendant be kept temporarily in custody or on bail, pending resumption of his case.
Repeal	The cancellation of a statute, or part of a statute, by another.
Reprieve	The suspension of execution of a sentence.
Riot	A tumultuous disturbance of the peace by three or more persons gathered together by their own authority mutually to assist one another against anyone who shall oppose them in the execution of some purpose, lawful or otherwise, and actually moving to execute that purpose violently to the terror of citizens.
Roll	Paper or parchment which may be turned or wound up.
Royal assent	Royal approval of a Bill which has been passed in both Houses of Parliament.
Sanctions	Penalties or punishments in disobedience of the law.
Scienter	Guilty knowledge; knowingly.
Serjeants-at-arms	Officers of the Crown; two of them execute the commands of each House of Parliament.

N

Serjeants-at-law	Barristers of a superior degree, now obsolete.
Scrivener	One who draws contracts; receives money to place at interest.
Search warrant	Granted by a magistrate or a judge to search premises under the authority of a statute, ie under the Theft Act 1968 to seek stolen property.
Sessions	Sittings of a court.
Sine die	(means 'without day'). Indefinitely; to adjourn a court without stating a day for meeting again.
Slander	Defamatory words, not in writing.
Status quo	The former state of things; to remain as they are.
Statutes	Acts of Parliament.
Sub judice	Under consideration by a court; it prevents discussion of the matter, eg in the press.
Submission	Putting a matter to the court; suggestions as to the law on a given set of facts.
Subpoena	(means 'under penalty'). A writ directing a named person to attend court and give evidence, under penalty for refusal.
Sue	To take legal proceedings in a civil court.
Suit	Civil legal proceedings. Civil actions at law.
Summary proceedings	Judicial proceedings before magistrates in petty sessions as opposed to trial before a jury.
Summons	A written order signed by a justice directing the person named there-

	in to appear at a given time, in the court named, with reference to the matter set out therein.
Supra	(means 'above'). Reference to a previous part of a book.
Testate	Having made a will.
Term	A sitting of the law courts.
Terminer	*See* Oyer and Terminer.
Testimony	The giving of evidence.
Thesaurus inventus	Treasure trove.
This day six months	Never. A proposal to read a Bill 'this day six months' means to reject it, ie Parliament will not sit six months hence.
Tipstaff	An officer of the high court in charge of the prisoners.
Tort	A civil wrong, not a breach of contract or trust. From *tortum* =wrested, wrung or crooked.
Trespass	Any transgression or offence against the law; interference with another's property, land or person.
Trial	Examination of a civil or criminal matter in a court of law.
Ultra vires	Beyond their powers or rights.
Usher	An official who keeps order and silence in court.
Venire de novo	(means 'to come anew')—a motion for a new trial.
Verderer	Forest official.
Verdict	The decision of a jury, civil or criminal.
Versus	Against. (Eg Brown versus Green, abbreviated to Brown v Green).
Vexatious litigant	A person bringing an action merely for spite, annoyance or oppression.

Void	Of no legal effect, a nullity.
Voidable	Something capable of being made void or even confirmed.
Waive	To forego; forsake; relinquish.
Warrant	A written authority signed by a justice directing the person to whom it is addressed to carry out the instructions therein, ie to arrest or search.

Bibliography

Abel-Smith, B. and Stevens, R. *Lawyers and the Courts*, 1967
Archbold's Criminal Pleading, Evidence and Procedure, 1969
Archer, P. *The Queen's Courts*, 1956
Baker, E. R. and Wilkie, G. H. *Police Promotion Handbooks No. 4 Administration and Organisation*, 1967
British Heritage. Odhams, 1948
Christian, R. *Old English Customs*, 1966
Cornish, W. R. *The Jury*, 1968
Counter, K. *The Framework and Functions of English Law*, 1968
Cross and Jones. *Introduction to Criminal Law*. 1967
Dale, Sir William. *The Law of the Parish Church*, 1967
Derriman, J. *Pageantry of the Law*, 1955
Devlin, J. D. *Criminal Courts and Procedure*. 1967
Garfitt, A. *The Book for the Police*, Vols 1–5, 1958
Giles, F. T. *The Criminal Law*, 1963
Hanbury, H. G. *English Courts of Law*, 1967
Havard, J. D. J. *Detection of Secret Homicide*, 1966
Holdsworth, W. S. *A History of English Law*, Vol 1, 7th Ed., 1956
Hooper, A. *Harris's Criminal Law*, 1968
Jackson, R. M. *The Machinery of Justice in England*, Cambridge, 1967
Jenkins, W. J. *The Courts of Justice*, 1967
Jenks, E. *A Short History of English Law*, 1949
Jervis Sir John. *The Office and Duties of Coroners*, 7th Ed.
Kenny, C. S. *Outlines of Criminal Law*, Cambridge, 1947

Kiralfy, A. K. R. *The English Legal System*, 1960
Lewis, J. R. *Civil and Criminal Procedure*, 1968
Mozley and Whiteley. *Law Dictionary*, 1962
O'Donnell, B. *Cavalcade of Justice*, 1951
Page, L. *Justices of the Peace*, 1967
Pasmore, A. *New Forest Commoners*, 1969
Radzinowicz, L. *A History of Criminal Law*, Vol 2, 1956
Report of the Royal Commission on Assizes and Quarter Sessions 1966–69 (Cmnd 4153), 1969
Smith, B. W. *The Wonderful Story of London*, 1949
Townsend, G. H. *The Manual of Dates*, 1867
Whiteside, J. *Hayward and Wright's Office of Magistrate*, 1953
Williams, G. *Learning the Law*, 1969

Index

Abbots, lords of the manor, 164; power to punish, 165
Abjuration of the realm, 106-7
Accidents, deaths, 104-5, 111-13, 116, 118-20; industrial, 113, 118; major, 120; road, 113, 119
Admiralty, 27, 79, 86, 94-6, 127, 150, 178; High Court of, 23, 86, 94-6
Adoption of children, 56, 79, 90
Affiliation orders, 56, 68
Affirmation, 12
Age of criminal responsibility, 70
Agisters, 161-3
Aid, see Legal Aid
Aldermen, 75; City of London, 27, 52
Alfred the Great, 83, 106
Anglicans, 12
Appeals, 125-38; against acquittal, 129; barred, 132; by battle (combat), 37, 125-6; case stated, 25, 135, 136-8, 147; certiorari (order of), 25, 120, 137; against conviction, 120, 130-1, 134, 142, 147; divorces, 92; early times, 84, 127, 176; ecclesiastical, 126-7, 165-8; errors of law, 18, 127-9, 131-2, 136; error (writ of), 128; false judgement (writ of), 127; judges of, 21, 129-30, 132, 134, 168; leave to, 21, 129, 131, 133-4, 143; legal aid, 139, 141-3; mandamus (order of), 25, 136; military courts, 21; Northern Ireland, 19; notice of, 130, 133, 135; pardon, 35, 132; prohibition (order of), 25; Scotland, 19; to sovereign, 84, 125-7, 150; tolt (writ of), 127; Wales, 19; witanagemot, 125; see also individual courts

Appeal, Court of, 19-22, 101, 125-38, 142, 147, 156
Appearance, entering an, 97
Appellate Committee, 21
Application to marry, 68
Archbishop, Canterbury, 165, 170; Hubert, 46; York, 18, 165, 167, 170
Archbishops' courts, 126, 165, 167-8, 170
Archdeacon's court, 126, 165
Arches, Court of, 167-9; Dean of, 89
Armorial bearings, 149
Array, challenge to, 42
Arrestable offences, 15
Arrests, 14-15, 46, 63, 146; by police, 14-15, 63, 146; by public, 15, 63
Articles of Eyre (1194), 103, 176
Assembly of the Wise, 17
Assize at Arms (1181), 57
Assize of battle, 37, 125
Assize of Clarendon (1166), 30, 36
Assizes, 16, 26, 28-45, 78, 84, 88, 91, 105, 119, 125, 129, 131, 153-4; appeals from, 125, 129; Bloody, 31; circuits, 29; commission of, 29, 31, 154; legal aid, 142; maiden, 33; origin, 30, 153; procedure, 33, 36, 41, 43, 131; Royal Commission on, 16, 28, 30, 58, 78-9, 151, 155-6, 158, 160, 164
Attachment, court of, 161ff
Aula, 174
Autrefois acquit, 35
Autrefois convict, 35

Bail, 143-8, 162; in appeals, 64, 135; in committal proceedings, 66; coroner's, 119, 145; excessive, 144; justices', 59, 144-5; police, 145; prison governor's, 145; procedure

for granting, 144-7; 'skipping', 148; sureties, 114-5, 147-8; young persons, 146-7
Bailiff's court, 75
Bankruptcy, 79, 80-3, 86, 148; appeal, 82; composition, 82; courts, 79, 80-3, 86; credit by, 83; discharge, 82; frauds, 81; procedure, 80, 82; punishment, 80-1; trustees, 82
Baptists, 12
Baron courts, 150
Barones of Exchequer, 170, 175-6, 182
Battle of Sluys, 94
Battle, trial by, 37, 125-6
Beck, Adolph, 141
Bench, Court of Queen's (King's), 21, 22-5, 84, 96, 127, 137, 139, 149, 160, 175, 177-9, 181; juvenile, 69-74; magistrates, 51, 54, 59, 64; Upper, 22
Betting licences, 50
Bill and answer, 180
Binding over, good behaviour, 57
Birdcage Walk, 26
Births (registration of), 109, 112-13
Bishop's court, 89, 126, 155, 165-6, 168
Bishop Williams, 85
Bloody Assizes, 31
Bodies, 105ff; definition, 111; not recoverable, 114; exhumation of, 111, identification, 115; see also Deaths
Bookmakers' licences, 50
Borough courts, 30, 75
Breach of the peace, 11, 57, 94, 150-1
Brodrick Committee on coroners, 121
Brougham, Lord, 77, 81
Brus, Robert de, 22
Buddhists, 12
Bullion, hidden, 122
Burgesses, Court of, 151
Burial, clubs, 110, order, 113
Buried treasure, 103-4, 122-4, 176

Cambridge University Court, 153
Canon law, 165-6, 169-70, 178
Canterbury, Archbishop's court, 126, 165, 167-8, 170
Canute, King, 75, 164
Care, protection and control (children), 69, 73

Casement, Sir Roger, 24

Case stated, 25, 135, 136-8, 147
Caveats, 88
Central Criminal Court, 25-8, 33, 41, 71, 95, 129ff
Certiorari, order of, 25, 120, 137
Challenges to Jury, 42
Chambers, judges in, 132
Chancellor, appeals to, 84, 128; origin of, 83; see also Lord Chancellor
Chance revenues, 104, 109, 122-3, 176
Chancery, appeals in, 86, 129, 154, 156, 167; Court of, 23, 81, 83-6, 88, 90, 154, 158, 175, 177-9, 182; Durham, 86, 153-4, 155-6; Lancaster, 86, 153-5; Masters in, 85, 155
Charles I, 85, 177, 181
Charles II, 128, 179
Chester (county palatine), 156
Children, see Juveniles
'Children's Charter', 69
Children's courts; see Juvenile courts
Chinese oath, 13
Chivalry, Court of, 149
Christian oath, 11ff
Church and state, 169-70
Cinque ports, 94
Civil appeals, see Appeal, Court of
Civil courts, 25, 32, 41, 43, 68, 75-101, 132-4, 139-41, 149ff
Classification of offences, 13-16, 60
Clergy, offences by, 169; punishment of, 169
Clifford, Lord de, 18
Coats of arms, 149-50
Codicil, 88
Coins, hidden, 122-4
College of Arms, 150
Combat, trial by, 37, 125-6
Commissary Court, 166
Commission, of assize, 29, 31, 154; of the peace, 32
Committal proceedings, 33, 56, 61-2, 121, 137, 142
Committee of Privileges, 21
Common Counsel of our Realm, 17
Common law, 9, 15, 70, 84, 95, 106, 111, 123, 129, 151, 153, 157, 169, 175, 181
Common Pleas, Court of, 23, 126-8, 155, 175, 177-9, 181
Companies, winding up of, 86
Compurgators, 36
Consistory Courts, 166-8
Conspiracy, 9

Constables, parish, 15, 38, 57, 151; petty, 57, 151
Contempt of court, 79, 149, 179
Contract, 25, 78, 95, 165
Contractual rights, 86
Conveyance, taking of, 15
Convocations, 169
Coroners, 102-24; abolition of, 121; appeal, 120, 131, 135; bail by, 119, 145; Brodrick Committee, 121; burial order 'pink form', 113; chance revenues, 104, 109, 122-3, 176; committal for trial, 67,110; conflict with rest of legal profession, 107-11; ex-officio, 102; fulltime, 102; homicide investigation, 110, 116, 119, 146; indictments, 18, 119, 121; jurisdiction of, 111, 113, 115-21; medieval duties, 103-107, 109, 114, 123, 176; police coroners' officers, 112, 117; police liaison, 110, 112, 114, 117; qualifications, 48, 102, 110; Select Committee on, 110; Society of, 110; sovereign, 102; treasure trove, 103-4, 122-4, 176; warrants, 18, 119, 121; see also Inquests, Deaths
Counter-claim, 97
Counties palatine, 153-6
County courts, 30, 75-80, 82, 88, 91, 151, 155, 158; appeal, 101, 125, 127, 134; circuits, 76; judges, 55, 77-9, 91; jurisdiction, 75, 77-8, 82, 88, 158; medieval, 30, 75, 155; origin, 75-6, 151; procedure, 41, 79
Courtesy, matters of, 149
Courts Christian, 165
Courts of conscience, 76
Courts leet, 150-2
Courts martial, 21, 150
Criminal appeal, see Appeal, Court of
Criminal responsibility, age of, 70
Cromwell, Oliver, 177
Crown Cases Reserved, Court of, 129
Crown Courts, Liverpool, 16, 28, 33, 55; Manchester, 16, 28, 33, 55; new, 16, 28
Crown pleas, custodian of, 103, 122
Curia Militaris, 150
Curia Regis, 83, 174-5, 177, 181; appeals, 175

Danby court leet, 152
Dangerous driving, 98, 120

Dean, Forest of, 162, 164; verderer's court, 162, 164
Dean of Arches, 89
Death penalty, 11, 14, 16, 24, 30, 31, 49, 81, 107, 114, 164-6, 180
Deaths accidental, 104-5, 111-13, 116, 118-20; certification, 109, 112-13; drowning, 108-9; enquiry into, 95, 103, 105, 108, 110, 115; in prison, 26, 104, 111, 114, 116; poisons, 109-10, 115-16; post mortems, 103, 108, 112-14, 118-19; unnatural, 105, 108, 110-12; see also Coroners, Inquests
Debtors, 77, 80-1, 88
Decree absolute, 92
Decree nisi, 92
Delegates, Court of, 127, 168
Demurrer, 34
Deodand, 104-6, 123
Depositions, 67, 119
Diocesan courts, 165
Diplomatic privilege, 111
Disasters, official enquiry into, 120
Divorce, 77, 79, 86, 89-94; appeals, 92; civil, 89; commissioners, 91; courts, 23, 86, 89, 90-4, 95; custody of children, 92; ecclesiastical, 89-90, 165; grounds for, 92-3; proceedings, 89, 91; publicity, 92; respondent, 91; undefended suits, 91-2
Domestic courts, 56, 58
Duchy of Lancaster (county palatine), 47, 77; Chancery Court, 86, 153-5
Dunmow Flitch, 152
Durham (county palatine), Chancery Court, 86, 153-4, 155-6

East India Company, 18
Ecclesiastical, appeals, 126, 166-8; courts, 88-90, 126, 150, 155, 164-70; 178; judges, 30, 83, 87, 155, 175, 178
Ecclesiastical Causes Reserved, Court of, 168
Edgar, King of Wessex, 57, 164
Edward the Confessor, 9, 75
Edward I, 17, 103
Edward III, 53, 87, 94, 125, 149, 152, 154, 179
Edward IV, 18, 151
Edward VI, 171
Edward VII, 26
Elizabeth I, 68, 81, 125-6, 128, 171, 182

Elizabeth II, 25
Englishry, proof of, 105
Entering an appearance, 97
Equity, 78, 84, 178
Error, 18, 127-9, 131-2, 136; writ of, 128
Estates, administration of, 86
Ethelred, 36
Evidence, hearsay, 100, 115; laws of, 37, 84, 92, 96-8, 100, 115
Examination in chief, 43, 65, 92, 100; post mortem, 103, 108, 112-14; 118-19; witnesses, 43-5, 65, 67, 92, 100
Examining magistrates, 56, 61, 66-8, 119, 137, 142
Exchequer, 17, 84; Chamber (Court of), 128, 182; Court of, 23, 83, 125, 128, 156, 170, 175-8, 181; of Pleas, 181
Excommunication, 165-6, 169
Executions, see Death Penalty
Exhumation of bodies, 111
Eyre, Articles of (1194), 103, 176; General, 29, 153, 161-2, 175-6

Faculty suits, 167-8
False judgement (writ of), 127
Family Division, High Court, 86, 90
Fawkes, Guy, 177
Felonies (felons), 14-15, 18, 30, 46, 81, 104, 153, 164, 180; abolition of, 15; forfeiture of goods, 14, 30, 104-7, 109, 123, 176
Fines, 59, 64, 73, 104-5, 116, 123, 152, 165
Fire of London, Great, 26
Fires, inquests on, 103
Forensic Science Laboratories, 115
Forest courts, 160-4; of Dean, 162, 164; laws, 161-2, New, 162-3; royal, 161
Forestry Commission bylaws, 163
Forfeiture of goods, see Felonies
Formal admission, proof by, 98
Franchise, Isle of Ely, 156; Palatine counties, 154
Frankpledge, courts of, 150

Game laws, 164
Gaming licences, 50
Gaunt, John of, 154
General Eyre, 29, 153, 161-2, 175-6
General gaol delivery, 32, 154
General issue, 36
George II, 32, 81
George III, 150

Gleasdale & Lealhome Association for the Prosecution of Felons, 15
Gold coins, trial of, 41, 170-3; hidden, 122, 124
Great Barmote Court, 152
Great Council, 17, 174, 178
Great Train Robbers, 9, 45
Greek Orthodox Church, 12
Grosvenor, Sir Robert, 150
Guardianship of infants, 56, 79, 90

Harclay, Sir Andrew, 150
Hearsay evidence, 100, 115
Henry II, 36-7, 103, 126, 170
Henry III, 157
Henry V, 47
Henry VI, 154
Henry VII, 179
Henry VIII, 47, 80, 87, 126, 150, 152, 155-6, 181
High Court, 17, 20, 82, 86, 95, 120, 133, 147, 155, 178, 182; Admiralty Division of, 94-6; Chancery Division, 23, 83ff, 86, 90, 182; of Delegates, 127, 168; of Parliament, 17, 19, 125
High misdemeanours, 180
Homicide, concealed, 102ff; investigation of, 110, 116, 119, 146
Honour matters of, 149
House of Lords, 17-22, 87, 90, 125, 128, 131, 134-5, 140, 142-3, 156, 170, 175, 182
Hubert, Archbishop, 46
Hue and cry, 57
Hundred Court of Salford, 78, 156
Hundredmen, 53
Hungerford Tutti-men, 152
Hunting, 160, 166
Hybrid offences, 60-1

Identification, inquest adjourned, 115
Impeachment, 19
Imprisonment, 69, 73, 81, 123, 151; magistrates' powers, 59, 62, 64, 73; suspended sentences, 64
Indictable offences, magistrates' courts, 56-7, 59-60, 62; 63ff, 67, quarter sessions, 53, 61-2; summary trial, 57-60, 62; trial of, 11, 24, 32, 33ff, 53, 56-63, 141, 150, 153, 180
Indictment, coroner's, 18, 119, 121; appeal from, 20, 131, 135; motion to quash, 34
Infants, bail by, 147; guardianship

of, 56, 79, 90; marriage of, 68;
wardship of, 86, 90
Inns, Serjeants', 128
Inquests, 102ff; adjournments, 115,
119; chance revenues, 104, 109,
122-3, 176; deaths, 102ff, 108-9,
111, 114; diplomatic privilege,
111, evidence at, 115; fires, 103;
fresh evidence, 120; identification
of persons, 115; juries at, 36, 38,
41, 104, 106, 115, 118, 120;
medical evidence, 108-10, 112-14,
117-18; procedure, 41, 67, 102,
111, 115-21; publicity, 117;
quashed, 120; riders, 120; treasure
trove, 103-4, 122-4, 176; verdicts,
118; see also Deaths, Coroners
Instance, Court of, 94
Interpreters, 13
Interrogatories, 98
Intestate persons, 87, 89
Isle of Ely, 156

James I, 81, 85
Jeffreys, Judge, 31
Jews, 12, 176, 179
Judges, Admiralty, 94-5; appeal
courts, 21, 129-30, 132; assizes,
30, 44, 142, 153-4, 176; county
court, 55, 77-9, 91; ecclesiastical
87, 178; errors by, 18, 127-8; ex-
officio, 27, 51, 160
Judicature, Supreme Court of, 23,
178
Jurisdiction, pleas to the, 35
Jurors, disqualified, 38, 39-40; exempted persons, 40-1; qualifications, 37-40, 48, 115
Jury, 15, 36-45; Admiralty, court,
96; challenge to, 42-3; Chancery
courts, 86; civil proceedings, 36ff,
39, 41, 86, 100, 134; common, 39;
county courts, 41, 79; courts leet,
151-2; criminal proceedings, 30
38, 41, 44, 54-5; empanelling, 41-
3; grand, 36-7; insufficiency, 43;
majority verdicts, 44-5; oath, 43,
116, 172; petty, 37; of presentment, 36; selection of, 37-40, 41,
48, 115; special, 39; trial by, 33,
41, 43, 61, 64, 66, 132, 136; Trial
of the Pyx 41, 170-3; verdicts, 44,
118; see also Inquests
Justice, Lord Chief, 27, 31, 102,
129-30, 149
Justice, Royal Courts of, 23, 86, 125,
177-8
Justice of the Peace Act (1361), 57

Justices of the Peace, see Magistrates
Juvenile courts, 12, 50, 56, 61, 68-
74; children in, 61; language in,
12, 72; permitted persons, 72;
press, 72; powers of, 61, 73;
venues, 72
Juveniles, age of criminal responsibility, 70; bail, 146-7; care, protection and control, 69, 73; definition
of, 70; divorce cases, 92; knowledge of wrong, 70

Keeper of the State Rolls, 85
Keepers of the peace, 46, 57
King's Bench, see Queen's Bench
King's Council, 17, 83-4, 95, 125-6,
171, 174, 179
King's Court, 10-11, 174-5; appeals,
18, 175
Knighthood, degradation from, 149
Knowledge of wrong, 70
Koran, 12

Lancashire Chancery Court, 86
Lancaster, Duchess of, 154; Duchy
of, 47, 77, 153-4; Duke of, 154
Law, canon, 165-6, 169, 178; common, 9, 15, 70, 84, 95, 106, 111,
123, 129, 151, 153, 157, 169, 175,
181; definition, 9; errors in, 128-9,
131-2, 136; forest, 161-2; game,
164; Poor, 68; Roman, 166, 169,
178; statute, 9, 10, 15, 18, 170,
181
Law Lords, 20-1
Laws of evidence, 37, 84, 92, 96-8,
100, 115
Leading questions, 110, 115
Leet, court, 150-2
Legal aid, 125, 138-43; appeals, 139,
141-3; assizes, 142; capital allowance, 139-40; charities, 139, 141;
civil cases, 138-41; civil courts,
90, 160; House of Lords, 140;
magistrates' courts, 140; quarter
sessions, 140; committees, 140-1;
contribution scheme, 142-3; criminal cases, 138, 141-3; ecclesiastical courts, 169; examining magistrates, 142; fund, 142; House of
Lords appeals, 140, 142-3; indictable offences, 141; magistrates'
courts, 140-2; newspapers, 139,
141; poor litigants, 78, 138-9,
175, 178; quarter sessions, 140,
142; Scotland, 138; summary
trial, 141; Tolzey Court of Bristol,
160

204 INDEX

Licences, betting operators, 50;
liquor, 50, 59, 102
Liverpool, Court of Passage, 78, 157-
8; Crown Court, 16, 28, 55
Long Parliament, 95
Lord Chancellor, 20-1, 27, 47-8,
50-1, 54, 80-1, 83, 85, 95, 128,
134, 171, 175, 182
Lord Chief Justice, 27, 31, 102, 129,
130, 149
Lord Lieutenants, 47
Lord Mayor of London, 27, 52, 79
Lords of Appeal in Ordinary, 21,
134, 168
Lords of the Manor, 150ff, 164, 174
Loughborough, Lord, 90
Lupus, Hugh, 156
Luther, Martin, 89
Lynch, Colonel Arthur, 24

Macclesfield, Countess of, 90
Magistrates, 46-74; administrative
capacity, 50, 57, 152; bench, 51,
54, 59, 64; boroughs, 48, 55;
chairman of, 49, 51; clerk to, 63;
constables, supervision of, 50, 57;
deputy chairman, 59; Duchy of
Lancaster, 47; early history, 46,
53, 57, 107; examining, 56, 61,
66-8, 119, 137, 142; ex-officio,
48-9, 51-2, 155; qualifications,
48-50; quarter sessions, 47, 53-4,
62; retired list, 48; supplemental
list, 48, training of, 50; women as,
48, 68-9, 72; see also Stipendiary
Magistrates.
Magistrates' court, 10, 41, 46, 56-
74, 91, 136-7, 140, 164; appeals,
25, 40, 64, 66, 131, 134, 136,
140, 147; bail, 59, 64, 66, 144-5,
147; case stated, 25, 135, 147;
children in, 61, 63, 73; civil
matters, 50, 54, 56, 68, 75, 91;
committal proceedings, 33, 56-7,
61-2, 64, 66, 121, 137, 142; committal for sentence, 62, 131, 135;
definition of, 58; development of,
56, domestic, 56, 58; jurisdiction,
50, 54, 56, 69, 75, 91, 136, 150,
164; juvenile, 12, 50, 56, 68-74;
legal aid, 140-2; licensing duties,
50, 56, 59, 102; matrimonial
cases, 56, 68, 91; occasional, 59;
offences triable at, 57-8, 60, 164;
procedure, 41, 58, 68; punishment by, 62, 64, 73; see also
Offences

Magna Carta, 17, 23, 87, 103, 138,
176-7, 180
Maiden assizes, 33
Majority verdicts, 44-5
Manchester Corporation, 149; Court
of Record, 156; Crown Court,
16, 28, 55; Palace of Varieties,
149
Mandamus (writ of), 25, 136
Manorial courts, 30, 47, 127, 150-2,
164
Maritime courts, 95, 157
Marriage, applications, 68, 176;
civil, 89-90; divorce, 89-94
Master of the Rolls, 85, 130
Masters in Chancery, 85, 155
Matrimonial cases, magistrates'
courts, 56, 68
Mayor's Court, City of London, 27,
79
Mayor's courts, 75, 159
Medieval county courts, 30, 75, 155
Metropolitan police courts, 56, 58,
72
Military courts, 21, 150
Mint, Royal, 106, 171-2
Misdemeanours, 14-15, 18, 24, 30,
123, 180; High, 180
Mohammedans, 12
Montfort, Simon de, 17, 46
Moravians, 12
More, Sir Thomas, 177
Morris, Lord, 38
Mortgages, 25, 86
Motion to quash indictment, 34
Motor Insurers' Bureau, 117
Murder, 14-15, 61, 108, 116; bail,
145; legal aid, 142-3; secret, 108ff

Naval courts, 94
New Forest, 160ff; agisters, 161-3;
court of swainmote and attach-
ment, 161-2; laws, 162; turbary,
163; verderers, 161-2
Newgate, 26
New Testament, 12
Nisi, decree, 92
Normans, murder of, 105
Norwich Guildhall Court, 78
Notice, to admit, 98; of appeal, 130,
133, 135; to produce, 98

Oath helpers, 36
Oaths, 11-13, 43, 65, 98, 100, 116,
172, 180
Occasional courts, 59
Offences, 11, 13-15, 60, 151; arrest-

able, 15; classification, 13, 60; felonies, 14-15, 18, 30, 104, 153, 180; hybrid, 60-1; matrimonial, 56, 68, 91; minor, 11, 60, 63, 151, 153; misdemeanours, 14-15, 18, 24, 30, 123, 180; poaching, 164; Summary, 58-62, 63ff; *see also* Indictable Offences
Official enquiries, 120
Old Bailey, 25-8, 33, 71, 95, 129ff
Old Newgate prison, 26
Old Testament, 12
Open verdicts, 118
Ordeal, trial by, 37, 125-6
Order, burial, 113; of certiorari, 25, 120, 137; of mandamus, 25, 136; of prohibition, 25
Ordinary, Court of, 166
Ore tenus, 180
Orthodox Churches, Greek, 12, Russian, 12
Outlaws, *see* Felonies
Oxford University Court, 152-3
Oyer and terminer, 31, 154

Palace of Varieties, Manchester, 149
Papal curia, 168
Pardon, 35, 132
Parish relief, 68
Parliament, 17, 175; Acts of, 9, 10, 15, 18, 170, 181; High Court of, 17, 19, 95
Partnership, 86
Passage, Court of, 78, 157
Pasturage, 161, 163
Pathologists, 115, 118
Peace, breach of, 11, 57, 94, 150-1; commission of, 32; conservators of, 57; justices of, *see* Magistrates; keepers of, 46, 57
Peers, trial by, 18
Pembrokeshire (palatine county); 11, 14, 16, 24, 30-1, 49, 81, 156
Peremptory challenge, 42
Pie Powder, Court of, 78, 158-60
Pipe rolls, 85, 103
Plate, gold and silver, 122
Pleadings, 96-7, 99
Pleas, 33-6, 154; common, 95, 126, 176, 181; Court of Common, 23, 126-8, 155, 175, 177-9, 181; custodian of Crown, 103, 122; demurrer, 34; Exchequer, 176, 181; to general issue (not guilty), 36; guilty, 33, 63-4; to jurisdiction, 35; in magistrates' courts, 63; minor civil, 76, 95, 176; special, 35

Poaching offences, 164
Police, commissioners of Metropolis, 50; coroners' liaison, 110, 112, 114, 117; courts, 56, 58, 72; prosecutors, 145
Polls, challenge to, 42
Pone (writ of), 127
Poor Law, 68
Poor litigants, *see* Legal Aid
Portmote, Liverpool, 157
Post mortem examination, 103, 108, 112-14, 118-19
Praemuniere, 127
Praying a tales, 43
Precedents, rule of, 85, 137
Press, coroner's court, 117; divorce courts, 92; juvenile courts, 72
Prison, children in, 69; deaths in, 26, 104, 111, 114, 116; Old Newgate, 26
Prisoners, antecedents, 33, 64, 66; guilty plea, 33, 63-4; not guilty plea, 33, 63-4; trial of, 33, 63-4, 104, 176, 180; unfit to plead, 33, 35
Privileges, Committee of, 21
Privy Council, 127, 168, 175
Prize court, 94
Probate, 86-7, 89, 95
Probate, Divorce & Admiralty Courts, 23, 86-96
Procurator Fiscal, 102
Prohibition (order of), 25
Protection, care and control children, 69, 73; Court of, 158
Provinces, York and Canterbury, 89, 165
Provincial courts, 89, 165; synods, 169
Purbeck Marblers, Court of, 152
Pyx, Trial of, 41, 170-3

Quakers, 12
Quarter sessions, 16, 26, 46-7, 53ff, 125; 136, 140, 151; appeals, 25, 54-5, 125, 129, 134, 136; bail, 145; borough, 55; chairman of, 77, 142; committal for sentence, 62, 131, 135; county, 54; jurisdiction of, 47, 53-6, 151; legal aid, 140, 142; London, 54; procedure, 33, 36, 41, 53ff; recorder, 33, 35; times of sitting, 53-4
Queen's (King's) Bench Division, 18, 22-8ff, 84, 88, 96, 125, 127, 137, 139, 149, 160, 175, 177-9, 181; civil jurisdiction, 22-5, 96, 139, 149; criminal jurisdiction, 24, 135; appeals, 21, 24, 125, 132

Queen's peace, 11, 57, 94

Realm, abjuration of, 106ff; Common Counsel of, 17
Reformation, 126, 168-9
Registrar, births and deaths, 109, 112-13; civil courts, 78-9, 81, 91, 97, 153, 155-7, 160
Reply document, 97
Reprieve, 132
Requests, Court of, 76, 178
Restrictive Practices Court, 158
Revenue, chance, 104, 109, 122-3, 176; royal, 84, 176, 181
Richard I, 103, 175
Richard II, 18, 85, 94-5, 150
Richard III, 144
Riders, coroner's jury, 120
Robbers, Great Train, 9, 45
Rolls, Master of, 85, 130; Pipe, 85, 103; Keeper of State, 85
Roman Catholic church, 12, 169
Roman law, 166, 169, 178
Royal fish, 104, 123
Royal Commission on Assizes and Quarter Sessions, 1966-69, 16, 28, 30, 58, 78-9, 151, 155-6, 158, 160, 164
Royal Courts of Justice, 23, 86, 125, 177-8
Rule of precedents, 85, 137
Russian Orthodox Church, 12
Ryedale court leet, 152

Sanctuary, 106-7, 164
Salford Hundred Court, 78, 156
Schyremotes, 75
Scrope, Sir Richard le, 150
Seaport courts, 94
Serjeant's Inns, 128
Settlements and trusts, 86
Shaftesbury, Lord, 85
Sheriff, 49, 75, 77, 103, 114, 127, 161, 166, 176; supervision of coroners, 103, 114
Ships, offences by crews, 11, 27, 95, 113
Silver coins, trial of, 41, 170-3; hidden, 122, 124
Sluys, Battle of, 94
Society of Coroners, 110
Special pleas, 35
Star Chamber, Court of, 178, 179-81
Stated case, 25, 135, 136ff, 147
Statement of claim, 96-7
State rolls, Keeper of, 85
Statute of Westminster (1275), 144

Statute of Westminster (1285), 87, 127
Statute law, 9, 10, 15, 18, 170, 181
Stipendiary magistrates, 48, 50-1, 52; indictable offences, 58; jurisdiction, 58; juvenile courts, 69; origin of, 50
Sturgeon, 104, 123
Summary offences, 58-62, 63ff
Summons, 63, 97, 159
Supreme Court, 20, 23, 125, 155, 178
Supreme Court of Justice for Greater Causes, 125
Suspended sentences, 64
Swainmotes, 161ff
Synods, provincial, 169

Tales, 43
Talesmen, 43
Tolt, writ of, 127
Tolzey Court, Bristol, 78, 158-60; Gloucester, 159; King's Lynn, 159;
Tort, 25, 78
Treason Act (1351), 24
Treasure trove, 103-4, 122-4, 176
Trial of the Pyx, 41, 170-3
Trinity House, 96
Trusts and settlements, 86
Turbary, New Forest, 163

Unanimous verdicts, 44, 173
Unfit to stand trial, 35
University courts, 152-3
Upper Bench, 22

Vatican, appeal to, 126, 168
Venison, 161
Verderers, 161-2; courts, 162, 164
Verdict, inquests, 118; majority, 44-5; open, 118; unanimous, 44, 173
Vert, 161
Victoria, Queen, 23, 106

Wapentakes, 57
Wards, 57
Wardship of infants, 86, 90
Water, trial by, 37
Weights and measures, 153, 176
Wessex, King of, 57, 164
Westminster Hall, 22, 30, 78, 84-5, 128, 175-9, 181
Whitehall, 175
Wilfred, Saint, 126
William the Conqueror, 9, 105, 155, 156, 165, 174
William IV, 81
Williams, Bishop, 85
Wills, 25, 86-9

Witan, 17
Witanagemot, 125
Worship, disturbance of, 18
Worshipful Company of Goldsmiths, 171
Wrecks, 86, 104, 123; Receiver of, 123
Writs, 84-5, 96, 154, 157, 159, 170, 180; error, 128; false judgement, 127; mandamus, 25, 136; pone, 127; tolt, 127
Wrong, knowledge of, 70

York, Archbishop of, 18, 165, 167, 170; Archbishop's court, 167
Young persons, *see* Juveniles